Napoleón Garcia & Analinda Dunn

The Genízaro
& the Artist

Stories from
New Mexico
Villages

Rio Grande Books

Stories from New Mexico Villages

Atarque: Now All is Silent by Pauliúne Chávez Bent

The Genízaro & the Artist by Napoleón Garcia & Analinda Dunn

Memories of Cíbola by Abe Peña

Villages & Villagers by Abe Peña

Other books of interest

Charlie Carrillo: Tradition & Soul by Barbe Awalt & Paul Rhetts

Nicholas Herrera: Visions of My Heart by Barbe Awalt & Paul Rhetts

Frank Applegate of Santa Fe by Daria Labinsky & Stan Hieronymus

Río Grande Books
Los Ranchos de Albuquerque, New Mexico

Napoleón Garcia & Analinda Dunn

The Genízaro & the Artist

*Stories from
New Mexico
Villages*

Published by Río Grande Books
www.nmsantos.com

Printed in the United States of America
Book design by Paul Rhetts and Barbe Awalt

Cover: Georgia O'Keeffe, Blue River (Chama River, Ghost Ranch, New Mexico), 1935, oil on canvas, 16 ½ x 30 ½ inches. Collection of the New Mexico Museum of Art. Gift of the Estate of Georgia O'Keeffe, 1987.

The path to the spot where the artist conceived this painting is worn daily by visiting tourists to Abiquiú. This is the most popular view shared by the artist with her admirers.

Library of Congress Cataloging-in-Publication Data

Garcia, Napoleón, 1931-
  The Genízaro & the artist / Napoleón Garcia & Analinda Dunn.
    p. cm. -- (Stories from New Mexico villages)

softcover ISBN-13: 978-1-890689-28-5 (1-890689-28-9)
hardcover ISBN 13: 978-1-890689-36-0 (1-890689-36-X)

  1. Garcia, Napoleón, 1931- 2. Abiquiú (N.M.)--Biography. 3. O'Keeffe, Georgia, 1887-1986--Homes and haunts--New Mexico--Abiquiú. 4. Folklore--New Mexico--Abiquiú. 5. Abiquiú (N.M.)--Description and travel. I. Dunn, Analinda, 1938- II. Title. III. Title: Genízaro and the artist.
  F804.A23G37 2008
  978.9'52--dc22
                              2008007586

The Genízaro
& the Artist

Napoleón Garcia, a native of Abiquiú,
New Mexico, tells about life in his
village and its most well-known
resident, world-renowned artist,
Georgia O'Keeffe

Contents

Napoleón Garcia, 2006. Photo by Analinda

Napoleón Garcia at work in his woodcarving studio, 2007. Photo by Analinda

Introduction

I have wanted to tell my story for many years. Actually I do tell it most every day as tourists find their way to my front porch that serves as both my tourist "office" and "gallery" for my woodworking. My house is right on the plaza in

Georgia O'Keeffe's Abiquiú Home viewed from below, near Highway 84. Glass window provided her a view of the Sangre de Cristo Mountains from her bedroom, 2006. Photo by Analinda

Abiquiú and I see many tourists come into our village, circle around and then head out. Some brave and curious ones make their way to my porch. I have been interviewed many times by journalists and authors who come to our village either to write about our traditional ways of living or to ask about one of our most famous residents, Georgia O'Keeffe, who made her home here in our village for over 40 years. However, I feel as if they look at us as curiosities of study or as actors in a living history park. I want to tell the story from the perspective of a native *Genízaro*, which are Hispanicized Indians of mixed breeds that were baptized by the Spaniards during the Colonial era of northern New Mexico. My ancestors participated in the original Spanish land grant that was granted to Abiquiú residents in 1754 and I was a neighbor of Miss O'Keeffe's for 40 years.

The village of Abiquiú is located in Rio Arriba County in Northern New Mexico, about 46 miles northwest of Santa Fe. This area is rich in history of the early Spanish colonization of New Mexico. Abiquiú sits right on the Spanish Trail that leads from Santa Fe to Los Angeles, California. This area has retained much of its early traditional ways due to its remoteness in the mountains of northern New Mexico. It has been only in the last half century that the outside world has discovered us. We even speak an archaic style of Spanish that consists of Colonial Spanish from Spain, some Mexican Indian words brought to us by the Conquistadors and words adopted from native Pueblo Indians. After Spain lost control of this area and Mexican control was far away we would even make up words for things that we had either forgotten their meanings or were new to our vocabulary.

In the last 10 years many people have come to our village in search of the home of the artist Georgia O'Keeffe and the country that inspired many of her paintings. Miss O'Keeffe started coming to New Mexico in 1929. She spent summers at Ghost Ranch, a dude ranch about 15 miles from the village of Abiquiú. She bought an old crumbling Colonial adobe home in our village in 1945 and had it remodeled to reflect its original style. After the death of her husband, Alfred Stieglitz, she moved permanently to our village and lived here for 40 years, right up until her death in 1986. She

Napoleón Garcia, The Abiquiú Genízaro Tourist Guide, 2007. Photo by Analinda

was my neighbor during this time and I had the privilege of working for her over the years. As a little kid I helped the men who were restoring her house, as a teenager and later as an adult I continued to work for her.

I want to tell the story of our village and how we accepted this world famous artist into our way of living. She became a "villager" here. She respected our way of life and had no desire to change us as so many outsiders want to do. She enjoyed our village customs and would participate in many of our events. O'Keeffe did everything she could to support and be part of the village, but she insisted that villagers do things their own way, saying, "I don't want to change you at all. That's why I moved here." I want to tell how she influenced the lives of some of our villagers. I also want to tell about my ancestors and the traditions that have been handed down and are still in use throughout our village today.

Georgia O'Keeffe at her Ghost Ranch home. Photo by John Loengard/Getty Images

Since my retirement I have been a tourist guide for this area. I love to tell people about my village and point them to the scenic areas that make this a most enchanting corner here at the end of the world. My schooling was very limited. I speak and write both Spanish and English—but neither very well. I am very grateful to my friend, Analinda. I told my story to her and she helped me to write it. We have put my story down as a series of short stories that reflect my life. When writing about my interactions with Miss O'Keeffe I use my nickname "Paul", because that is what she called me, however, I much prefer to be called Napoleón.

Georgia O'Keeffe in the garden at the Abiquiú home. Photo by John Loengard/Getty Images

Pastoral view of Cerro Pedernal from Ghost Ranch, 2006. Pedernal appeared in many O'Keeffe paintings and continues to be captured in contemporary paintings and photographs. Photo by Analinda

The Ditch

The artist lady came out of her adobe house into the yard where the young Genízaro boy was digging the fresh spring earth for her garden.

"Paul, why does it take so many men and so many days just to clear a narrow ditch for the water?"

All property owners had been requested to send one man to help with the annual clearing of the irrigation ditch, or acequia, that brought the precious water from the mountain spring into the village. The artist lady had released one of her workers right at the time when she needed to get her garden ready for spring planting. Paul attempted to explain the required ritual of clearing the winter damage from the ditch. The lady listened without comment, turned and re-entered the house only to return wearing her wide brim hat, and sturdy walking shoes.

"Show me this ditch, Paul."

The young man put down his tools and began walking with the lady up the dusty road, past the scattered adobe homes, past the old cemetery, up into the canyons, following the narrow two-foot ditch that carried the source of life to this thirsty, high desert village in northern New Mexico.

The irrigation ditch was one of the legacies handed down to the villagers from their ancestors who had settled there centuries ago. The Abiquiú Land Grant of 1754 was one of the few Spanish Land Grants made to Genízaros, people of mixed Indian and Spanish ancestry. The village was surrounded by natural springs with one main source high in the surrounding mountains.

Each year after the winter rains the men of the village would walk the ditch, making any required repairs caused by the snow and rains. The Majordomo, *the appointed man in charge, a position that would rotate among the villagers from year to year, used a measuring stick marking off each section to be worked and then assigning that section to a worker. The men worked their section, then helped others finish their assignments before the* Majordomo *would again use his stick and mark off*

Abiquiú Plaza viewed from Moquí. This church replaced the earlier church that burned in the 1880s. A few of the buildings still exist around the plaza. Photo by T. Harmon Parkhurst, ca.1915; courtesy Palace of the Governors (MNM/DCA), Negative Number 13698.

the next assigned areas. This was a process that had been used for centuries and the villagers had no need to improve or change how things had worked before.

Soon Paul and the lady came to the area of the ditch that had been cleared. It was evident that much soil and rocks had been recently removed from the channel. They walked further up the arroyo until they came to the working men. The lady stood watching for a while without comment until she seemed satisfied that this was indeed a necessary endeavor and turned to leave the men to their ancient tasks.

On their return back to her house she would stop every so often and gaze out over the valley.

Abiquiú Plaza viewed from Moquí, 2007. Photo by Analinda. Photo taken from the yard of Napoleón's boyhood home. The Catholic Church of St. Tomás the Apostle is the third church built on this site. Labor to build the church was volunteered by villagers and valley men and women. The Church was completed in 1937. The tumble-down adobe house to the far right can be seen again in the 1915 photo of the plaza—only in a little better condition.

"I never tire of this view, Paul". "Shapes and colors can change each time you look at the same thing."

Paul was used to these breaks to absorb the breathtaking beauty of the blue hills and mesas. The lady often asked him to walk with her as she hiked the hills and canyons surrounding the village of Abiquiú. When they returned to her house the lady said no more about the ditch-digging efforts and Paul returned to his tasks in the garden.

∾ ∾ ∾ ∾ ∾ ∾

I was 14 when Miss Georgia O'Keeffe bought the old colonial adobe in my village of Abiquiú. It took about four years for her to renovate the crumbling structure. She moved permanently to the village in 1949, after settling the affairs in New York of her late husband, Alfred Stieglitz. She had been coming to New Mexico since 1929. She began staying at Ghost Ranch, a dude ranch popular for Easterners at that time, which is about 15 miles northwest of Abiquiú. In 1940 she bought one of the summer homes at the ranch. She would live at both residences until her death in 1986.

She wanted the house in the village of Abiquiú because she desired to have a garden. During the war years it was necessary for people to be more self-sufficient in providing their food, especially in this remote section of northern New Mexico. She also had a craving for fresh fruits and vegetables that could not be satisfied by infrequent trips over the rutted road into Española, 22 miles away. The house in Abiquiú came with the very desirable water rights. I think she also desired to live among the native people of the village who were quite unlike the "dudes" that came to vacation at Ghost Ranch. She had expressed her dislike more than once for these "dudes" who came west to be temporary cowboys.

Her interest in our methods of maintaining the irrigation ditch is but one example of her interest in our way of doing things. Here she was, a lady of the city, who probably thought nothing of turning on the tap to have water run freely in her home. She wanted to understand why this annual effort was so important to our village's way of life. I think after she saw how we cleared the ditch without using machinery, using only the determination of the villagers to maintain a life-giving legacy of their ancestors, she was impressed and satisfied without wanting to change how we did things. Most people would want to suggest our getting earthmoving equipment in or perhaps hiring a professional company who could install more permanent culverts that could withstand the winter's onslaught. But Miss O'Keeffe accepted our way life style. I think this is why she wanted to live in our village. We accepted her and she accepted us as we were without wanting to bring in all the newer technologies that were changing, some think *improving*, the way of life in the cities. The ditch continues to be maintained by the villagers.

Storm over Ghost Ranch. Much-painted red and yellow cliffs by Georgia O'Keeffe, 2006. Photo by Analinda

Some villages have elected to line their ditches or *acequias*, with cement. They thought it was too much trouble to clean it out each year. The cement would keep the water from seeping into the ground on its way to irrigate their gardens. First, the small plants would die that used to line the waterway. There would be no more fresh watercress to spice and freshen their food. Then, the thirsty cottonwoods, that depended on the seeping waters, would die away. When the plants left the birds and animals would soon follow. Soon the area would be a dead zone. Not only was nature destroyed, but the village culture would be greatly changed. Some villages would make an annual celebration of the ditch cleaning and the priest would bless the water before irrigation began each spring. But these traditions have vanished in many villages. It was too much

Abiqueños celebrate their Spanish heritage during the Santa Rosa de Lima Fiesta in August. Celebrations start with Mass at the ruins of the old church on Highway 84; 2007. Photo by Analinda

of a problem to clean the *acequias*, too much of a problem to maintain their culture. It's as if they just turned their backs to tradition and walked away, in different directions, further apart from their community and each other. I'm very proud that Abiquiú did not follow this route. We still maintain and share the maintenance and use of our waterway.

I must include an early recollection about the irrigation ditch. Along the route the water had to travel over an arroyo. The ancestors had built a trestle for a trough over the arroyo so that the water could continue on its path. Replacing the wooden trestle and trough was the only periodic improvement required over the years. In later years the wooden trough was replaced with a permanent metal culvert.

As a young boy I remember my friends and I would play in the wooden trough. One kid would sit in the trough,

After the Mass, the Saint is taken by procession to the village and placed in a bower on the Abiquiú Plaza, then the fiesta begins, 2006. Photo by Analinda

diverting the water over the side so that others could play in the makeshift waterfall below. When the flow of water was slowed or stopped by our body-dam the men from the village would start to walk the path of the ditch to find the cause of the reduced flow. When the men found the cause of the stoppage, they would see a bunch of naked kids down below, running to find their clothes for a quick getaway. Perhaps there was more than one reason to replace the open trough with a culvert.

Before we had water lines into our homes, the village would use water from the surrounding creek or springs for drinking. Getting water in buckets from the creek or springs near the village was always a good job for the children. A ditch was dug to divert water from the main ditch to a pond

Abiqueños celebrate their Indian heritage during the St. Tomás Fiesta in November, 2006. Photo by Analinda

up above the village in the old ancient Hopi site of Moquí. But this pond was only for use in the summer because in the winter it would freeze. It was my job to carry buckets of water from the pond to the house for our use. There was a huge log across the pond from which I would dip my bucket into the pond to fill with the clear water from the center of the pond. More than once I would slip and fall head first into the pond.

The springs, creek and a few wells were winter sources of water. I was raised in Moquí. When I was young and the pond

Brothers Jackie Suazo and Napoleón Garcia celebrate their Indian heritage at a St. Tomás Fiesta. Garcia Family Photo

was dry or frozen I would have to go down to the creek for water. This was a big job for a little guy. Often I would have to return and refill buckets that had been spilt as I climbed the wintry-slick hill.

We were one of the first communities in this region to have water brought into our houses for drinking and sanitation. Miss O'Keeffe was instrumental in getting this done. When we applied to the government for help we were told to put up half the money in order to get it done. Miss O'Keeffe stepped in and provided the funds that the village was required to pay. This water comes from the same source as our irrigation water, but is tapped at the source and carried by pipes into our homes.

The water management and maintenance is administered by a committee of Abiquiú residents. Sometimes if the lines are damaged by storms or they are constructing new lines to new homes the water may be shut off for a long period of time. The wise Abiquiú resident will have many bottles of water stored just in case of this type of emergency need. If you looked in my kitchen right now you would see a variety of water-filled bottles lining the counter near my sink. My children know where to come for water if this need arises.

The Hunger

"Come on, Jackie, if you are going with me today."

Young Paul was on his way down from his home up in Moquí, the ancient village that stood above the newer settlement of Abiquiú. The artist lady had asked him to come and repair some of the adobe walls surrounding her home at the edge of the village. Sometimes his younger brother, Jackie, would tag along. It seems as if the artist lady had taken a liking to the younger Genízaro boy and would sometimes let him paint in her studio.

The two boys walked the dusty paths down from their home, through the plaza, past the newly rebuilt Church of Santo Tomás, built in the classic Pueblo-mission style, with labor volunteered by village and valley men in 1938. The home of the artist lady stood on the edge of the mesa that contained the village of Abiquiú. It looked over the Chama River Valley, eastward, with the Sange de Cristo Mountain Range in the far distance. The home was built in the early years of the 19th century by General José María Chávez, a Mexican General who commanded troops in Abiquiú during the Mexican occupation of New Mexico and later became a General with the United States when Mexico lost control of the area. The home was built in the Spanish Colonial style that was popular at that time. It had taken the artist lady over ten years to secure the purchase of the home from the Archdiocese of Santa Fe. At the time of purchase the home had been used to house the village livestock. Much renovation was required before the house was habitable.

The boys entered the garden gate, ignoring the "Beware of Dog" sign hanging there. The Chows owned by the lady were well accustomed to the boys and welcomed their entry with enthusiastic wagging tails. Jackie peered inside until he caught the attention of the artist lady and was invited into her studio,

Paul worked away mixing the mud and slathering it onto a few cracks that had appeared in the garden wall. He liked working in the well-kept garden where trees bore succulent fruit and colored vegetables peeked from under well-maintained green foliage. Paul's family rarely had an abundance of any type of food. This Garden of Eden was a mouth-watering paradise to him. Of course the garden walks were lined with the flowers that the artist lady loved to paint.

The artist was showing Jackie how to mix paints when she decided that perhaps he would like a snack.

"Jackie, let's take a break and go into the kitchen and get a bite to eat."

When they were seated the cook turned to them and said, "I'll feed you," she said to the artist lady, "but I am not feeding him."

With this statement the cook waved her arm, indicating the Genízaro boy sitting with the artist lady. The silence hung heavy over the table but was soon broken by the lady who fired the cook on the spot, then continued to prepare the meal herself.

It was a shock to the artist lady that someone from the very village where the boy lived could be so hurtful to the child, let alone be so arrogant to her employer. The boys, however, were far too used to this type of treatment from their fellow villagers. They tried not to let episodes such as this hurt them. However, the sting, felt not only in their stomachs but in their hearts, would remain forever.

Brothers Norman Suazo and Napoleón Garcia modeling clothes made by their Mother, 1936. Garcia Family Photo

∾ ∾ ∾ ∾ ∾ ∾

We were considered the outcasts of our village. I was born in Santa Fe where my father had gone in search for work during the Depression year of 1931. Within a very short time my mother, Lucia Suazo, came back to Abiquiú with my three-year-old brother, Nelson, and me. My father had abandoned us and my mother, who was unable to speak, read, or write English, had to return to her home village. She was disowned by her own parents for having children out of wedlock and was shunned by my father's family, the Garcias, and the rest of the village. We squatted in empty adobe huts, cooking in fireplaces and drawing water from the nearby creeks and springs or from neighbor's wells when they would let us. My mother earned what money she could by plastering adobe buildings and doing laundry for people who could pay. We only ate when she could manage to scrounge supplies for a few beans and *tortillas*. Summers were better when we could forage for food in the mountains, gathering *quelites* (wild spinach), *guaco* (Rocky Mountain bee plant), *chimajá* (wild parsley), wild asparagus and the watercress that grew near the streams.

We slept on pallets on the floor, covering ourselves with cardboard to keep out the cold. When it rained we would cover the cardboard with oilcloth to keep our makeshift bedding dry. We dressed in cast-off adult clothing that my mother could cut down to fit. Shoes were the biggest problem. I can remember when my mother persuaded me to wear a pair of ladies' black flats to school saying that the kids wouldn't notice. I fled from school in tears chased by the merciless teasing of the other kids.

We didn't have running water, so in addition to being hungry we were almost always dirty. We were allowed, but not encouraged, to attend the village elementary school. However, the teachers didn't really want us there. I was never very good with reading or writing in school. I speak both

Spanish and English, but neither one very well. I did like numbers and could do the math. One time I had completed a math homework assignment and handed it in with pride. I had made 100% but the teacher didn't believe that I had done the work myself so she did not give me credit for the work.

Lucia Suazo with young Jackie Suazo, 1936. Garcia Family Photo

I never felt as if I belonged in school. I barely completed the elementary grades.

There were some kids who were fortunate enough to have help with their homework. I never could understand how a close friend of mine did so well in school. He always had his homework completed and correct. He did very well on tests. He was a year behind me, then caught up with me and soon was promoted on to the next grade. In later years I found out that during this time of his acceleration in school, the teacher was rooming at his house and was tutoring him at night. I had no one to help me at home because when my mother went to school she was taught in Spanish and I was being taught in English.

We were outcasts in our own village. Some people showed kindness but most were very cruel. When we walked from our home in Moquí we had to pass in front of a home where two old spinster ladies lived. When they saw us coming they would throw their hot waste-water on or near us, splashing us or causing us to walk through the muddy road. Other times they would throw discarded food in the road in front of us. I never knew if they were offering us food or just showing us that they had food to throw away. I think it was the latter. They knew we were always hungry and this was their way to humiliate us.

People would call us "bastards" and kick and chase us from their doors. Too many times I would be playing with the village children in the plaza when they would be called home for a snack, a meal or even a festive party and I would be told to wait outside or to go away until the meal was over.

Slowly things began to improve after my mother's father died. A reconciliation of sorts was made with our maternal grandmother, who lived in the village of Barranco, about two miles from Abiquiú. We weren't allowed to live with her but we did get to know her and she gave us food sometimes. Mother began working more steadily as a mud plasterer and

Brothers Norman Suazo and Napoleón Garcia at their First Communion, 1939. Garcia Family Photo

laundress for Miss O'Keeffe. This was when Miss O'Keeffe took an interest in me and my brother and hired us to do odd jobs around her house.

The fact that I have survived and can tell this story is owed totally to my mother. She lived to be 103. I was glad in later years to see her provided for by her children. She colored her hair to her dying day and even though she was the senior-most resident in the home where she lived her last days, she always complained about all "those old people" living with her.

One time Miss O'Keeffe called me to come in and have a glass of milk or some other refreshment. As I had in other times when she made this offer, I declined, saying "No thank you, Miss O'Keeffe. I am not hungry." But this time she stopped me and ordered me to come into the kitchen. She asked why I always refused her offer for refreshment when she knew that I had been working hard and must be hungry. The only truthful answer was I was not used to being offered snacks or food when I was working and I didn't trust the sincerity of the offer.

Pains of hunger haunt me to this day. If for any reason when I go without food, the hunger pangs normally felt will bring these deep-seated hurts and fears to the surface. I always have food in my house for my marauding children and grandchildren when they come. They know not to walk past the refrigerator without checking in to see what I might have stocked for them to pillage. Additionally, I am very careful how I treat children. Being the father of ten gave me lots of practice. I know only too well that treatment given to children, even teasing by adults, can scar and remain with them for a lifetime.

Miss O'Keeffe's cook had shown her dislike for us at other times. When we were working outside, many times we would have to go in and out to get tools or carry things back and forth. She would often come and lock the gates behind us

Georgia O'Keeffe recognized the artistic talent in Napoleón's brother, Jackie Suazo. He continued with his art and became a notable artist in Santa Fe. Garcia Family Photo

forcing us to walk all the way around the house to continue our work.

As I looked back to the incident when Miss O'Keeffe fired the cook for slighting her young guests, I like to think that it was out of charity for us that she felt this way and not because the servant spoke arrogantly to her employer. Other times Miss O'Keeffe's generosity might come under question. Once when I was her chauffer I had driven her to a meat market in Santa Fe to get meat for her beloved Chows. She had choice meat cut from the bones and packaged for her canine friends. I could easily have used the bones to make a soup base for my growing family, but the butcher gave them a toss into a nearby bucket of scraps. We left with a big bag of prime meats. When we returned to Abiquiú I had secretly hoped that perhaps Miss O'Keeffe would give me one of the steaks to take home, but to her it was only "dog food".

This incident is still with me. That meat market is no longer operating in Santa Fe. It is now some other store, but every time I pass it I recall that day devoted to buying meat for her dogs. In our old age we are supposed to be forgetful. I wish sometimes I could forget some of these early occasions of my youth. But the scars are too deep and it only takes a little brush of memory to bring them to the surface again.

Another time I drove her to Taos for shopping. We stopped at a clothing store and while she was shopping I looked around. She saw me admiring some sweat pants and said, "Go ahead, Paul. Get yourself those pants."

"No, Miss O'Keeffe, I only have a few dollars and I really shouldn't spend them on these pants."

"Go on, get them, I'll pay for them. I'll reimburse you for them when we return to Abiquiú."

But, she never did.

*O'Keeffe, Georgia. From the White Place 1940, Oil on canvas 30 x 24 in;
76.2 x 60.96 cm. Acquired 1941 The Phillips Collection, Washington, DC
© 2007 The Georgia O'Keeffe Museum/ Artists Rights Society (ARS), New
York*

Abiqueños call it Plaza Blanca *or the White Cliffs. Georgia O'Keeffe referred
to them as "the White Place". These white cliffs are highly visible from the
village of Abiquiú. Anyone visiting Abiquiú is sure to notice these cliffs in the
distance on the north side of the Chama River. This area is on the grounds
of Dar al Islam Mosque. The mosque is opened to the public and the area is
available for hiking.*

Georgia O'Keeffe, American, 1887-1986, Black Cross, New Mexico, 1929. Oil on canvas, 99.1 x 76.2 cm. Art Institute Purchase Fund, 1943-95 Reproduction, The Art Institute of Chicago

Even though Georgia O'Keeffe did not practice any established religion she had a great reverence and admiration for the Pentitentes of New Mexico, their moradas and their use and display of the cross. She painted several of their crosses.

Georgia O'Keeffe, My Backyard, 1937 ca. 1916, New Orleans Museum of Art: Museum purchase, City of New Orleans Capital Funds, 73.8 © 2007 The Georgia O'Keeffe Museum/ Artists Rights Society (ARS), New York

These unique red and yellow cliffs are behind the O'Keeffe home at Ghost Ranch. This area is easily recognized by today's visiting artists who try to capture the magic of this landscape just as Georgia O'Keeffe did.

Near Abiquiú, New Mexico - Hills to the Left, 1941. Georgia O'Keeffe (1887-1986) Oil on canvas, © 2007 The Georgia O'Keeffe Museum/ Artists Rights Society (ARS), New York. 12 X 30 inches. Photograph courtesy Spanierman Gallery, LLC, New York

The Abiquiú landscape was featured in many of O'Keeffe's paintings

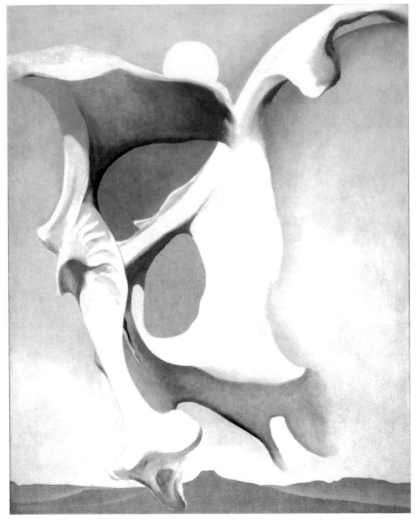

Pelvis with the Moon-New Mexico, 1943. Georgia O'Keeffe. Oil on canvas 30 x 24 in. Purchase, the R.H. Norton Trust, 58.29. Norton Museum of Art, West Palm Beach, Florida.

Many times when driving Miss O'Keeffe, Napoleón would have to stop and load animal bones into the car. Abiqueños considered this bone collecting habit of the artist very strange.

Again, the artist didn't let this opportunity pass without including her favorite mountain, Cerro Pedernal, in the painting.

The Differences

It was a hot summer day and Paul had been working hauling topsoil across the artist lady's garden. The ever-expanding garden enclosed by the adobe wall surrounding the old Colonial home of the artist, was a place of pride and joy for Paul to work. He had helped his Uncle Esteven plant the many fruit trees and he enjoyed watching them take hold in this high desert climate and bear fruit.

The artist had been watching him work from her window. She came out into the yard and said, "Paul, I've been watching you work. Why do you come back with an empty wheelbarrow after you dump the soil? Fill your wheelbarrow with those rocks that need to be taken out. This way there is no wasted efforts."

"I've been working all day. It is hot and I've already moved a mountain of dirt," replied the weary Paul.

"Well, I think you are wasting time and effort by pushing an empty load half the time. I want you to move those rocks," the lady said.

Paul rarely expressed his anger, but this time with sweat rolling off his brow and muscles aching from a full days labor, said, "Slave times are over, Miss O'Keeffe. I'm not your slave."

"Move those rocks or you are fired," replied the lady who rarely gave in to an argument.

"You can't fire me, Miss O'Keeffe, because I quit!" replied

the Genízaro *youth whose stubborn nature made a good match to the fiery independent lady.*

"Well, go on home, then," sparked the artist lady.

"OK, I'll go home. I have a poor, old adobe home. That's where I'll go," replied the equally fired-up young man.

With this reply, Paul lowered the empty wheelbarrow to the ground and walked out the garden gate and to his home. The next day the artist lady was knocking on his door. Without an apology, she said, "Paul, let's forget all about yesterday. I need you to finish that job."

Paul returned to the task. This was only one of many instances when the two people, artist and worker, would come to differences that caused temporary firings, only to be rehired. Never were the differences discussed nor were apologies given.

∾ ∾ ∾ ∾ ∾ ∾

This is but one of the instances when I would clash with Miss O'Keeffe. We would often disagree about how something should be done, ending in my being fired and later rehired. She never would discuss these differences and never offered an apology for what I think was her discriminating nature toward me. She obviously thought I was a "lazy *Genízaro*" taking advantage of her employment by working only half the time by not pushing a full load with each step I took.

She had a very good memory. She knew exactly which pear was ripe and how many strawberries were ready for picking. I would come to work in the early morning. I was young and hungry and I just might help myself to that pear or eat a handful of ripe, red berries as I worked. She would come out and say, "Paul, did you eat that pear?" or "There were a bunch of berries ready to be picked, did you eat them?"

Of course I would always confess that I had indeed eaten the fruit. She never commented one way or the other about my helping myself to her produce, but it was apparent that she wanted me to know that she was watching me. Not only was I a lazy *Genízaro*, I was a thieving one, also. She knew that I was living a very poor existence and perhaps I had not eaten that morning before I came to work, but at that given instant she only saw a *Genízaro* stealing from her garden.

At times she was very aware and concerned in her own way about the living conditions of my family. She knew how the villagers treated us and how my mother was trying hard to keep her little family fed and clothed. She had become quite fond of Jackie and was concerned about the treatment he was receiving at school. She went to the priest so he could translate into Spanish her offer of adoption or perhaps sending Jackie to Boys Town. At that time Boys Town in Nebraska was a haven for orphaned boys who were without families and lost in the economic difficulties caused by the Depression years.

As the priest explained her offer my mother quickly replied, "No, my son is not a piece of *tortilla*. I'm not going to give him away to go somewhere else. So, go away! Get out of here!" With this bold statement she chased the priest and artist from her door.

Miss O'Keeffe was blind to the family bonds that existed and could not understand how important it was to my mother to succeed in raising her children in spite of the treatment shown by family and villagers. You might be able to see where my stubbornness comes from.

Miss O'Keeffe bestowed no special treatment on me. My brother Jackie was not only younger than me but he was shorter and smaller. I was nearly full-grown at age 15 and towered at over six feet. In her eyes I was a grown man and good for working. Jackie had shown his talent for painting and she was instrumental in helping him. He went on to become a recognized artist in Santa Fe.

In her own way, Miss O'Keeffe did a lot for our village. She insisted on building a gymnasium for the youth of the village. Even if her ulterior motive was to have a handsome tax reduction, she did show favor to the young people of Abiquiú.

Additionally, she loaned us $10,000 to complete the interior of the gymnasium. She requested that we repay her $1000 each year. When the committee presented the yearly check to her she would make note of it as payment; then turn around and sign the check back over to us for expenses or further improvements on the gym. I can't say that she was an overly generous person. She would always maintain some type of control over the "gifts" she bestowed on us. Many people in the village would approach her for money. Most were turned down. Often the villagers would seek either me or my brother Jackie, to go with them or be part of their "committee" when they were seeking her financial assistance because they knew that she had shown favoritism to us growing up. However, I cannot say I was ever her pet; maybe Jackie was, but not me. I was her good, hard worker

Once when her sister was visiting I would drive the sister around in her big car that she had brought from California. When the sister was to return to California she asked me to drive her back and then she would fly me home. This sounded like a great adventure for a young man like me who had never left Abiquiú! But when Miss O'Keeffe heard of the plan it was quickly changed to another young driver in the village. I think Miss O'Keeffe wanted to keep me there in case she needed me for work. She didn't stop to consider that a trip like that would be something I would enjoy.

Another time, while driving her past some of the poor nearby pueblos, I commented on how desperate some of these people lived, huddled in mud huts, never knowing where the next meal would come from.

"That's all they need, Paul," responded Miss O'Keeffe. "That's what they are used to. They wouldn't know what to do with more or better conditions. That's the way they want to live."

"Oh, no, Miss O'Keeffe," I quickly replied. They *do* want better things just like all of us. Who would *want* to live like that? They all dream of a better life."

A friend of mine, who was raised in the deep southern state of Alabama during the same years of my youth, remarked that this reminded her of how the blacks were treated before the effects of the civil rights action of the 1960s. She, too, grew up thinking that the blacks *wanted* to live the way they did. They had their special day to come into town to shop. It was rare to find white people shopping in town on Saturday. My friend grew up thinking that Saturday was for getting ready for church the next day and wouldn't even think of going to town for any reason. The blacks had their own cafes and "honky-tonks", always on the edge of town and where no white person would ever venture. They had their private entrance in the alley to the town's one and only movie theater. There they would buy their tickets, walk down the dark alley, then climb the stairs to sit in the balcony. My friend always thought that this was what the blacks wanted—including separate bathrooms and drinking fountains. To this day she says it is hard for her to sit in a balcony of any theater.

I have seen my grandchildren suffer from acts of discrimination. My granddaughter was driving across country from Mississippi to New Mexico. This was after September 11, 2001 and she was stopped, pulled over and questioned as she attempted to cross a bridge that was heavily guarded against terrorism. My granddaughter is a tall, blond, anglo-appearing young lady, but she was a suspect because her identification bore the last name of *Garcia*.

I always get a good laugh when reading the monthly section in the *New Mexico* magazine titled "One of Our Fifty is Missing." People write in and tell how their living in New Mexico has been interpreted as living *outside* of the United States. It usually involves ordering online or over the phone, and when giving their address they are informed that the company does not ship out of the U.S. It happens often enough for this to be a regular, monthly section in the magazine. Once when I was traveling I jokingly asked a cashier if she would take New Mexican money. At first she said "no", but then looked confused when I handed her U.S. bills.

I heard once that the name *Smith* is no longer the most prevalent name in America's phone books. It has been replaced by the name *Martinez*. However, attitudes are slow to change. I've lived with these discriminating acts all of my life, but I think that in some ways it is getting worse due to the recent surge in immigration problems and border concerns.

Miss O'Keeffe was a woman of her time. Some people call this "unconscious discrimination". It is a trait that is engrained in us from generation to generation; and, even after the turbulent 1960s, our society is still reluctant to accept all people on an equal basis.

Chama River in Fall, 2006. Photo by Analinda

Chama River in Winter, 2007. Photo by Analinda

Chama River running through the farming area known as Sylvestres, just north of Abiquiú. The Abiquiú Mesa can be seen in the background, 2006. Photo by Analinda

Cerro Pedernal Frosted with a Late April Snow, 2006. Photo by Analinda

The *Penitentes*

Paul had walked down to the artist lady's home soon after dawn on this bright spring morning to finish some garden preparations that he had started earlier in the week. Spring had come early to this small pueblo village of Abiquiú high on a mesa, overlooking the Chama River Valley in northern New Mexico. As he walked, the apricot and peach blossoms fluttered in the wind like downy snowflakes making a snowy path for him to tread. The lady artist dearly loved her garden and was anxious to get started with this promise of an early spring.

Later, as Paul was turning the soil in the garden, he could hear the shrill notes of a flute off in the distance. This was soon followed by the sound of many masculine voices chanting in unison. This was the start of a procession of the Hermanos de la Luz, Brothers of the Light, a Penitente group that had been established in Abiquiú over 400 years earlier. The Penitentes were marching from their Morada del Alto, located up the dusty road from the old Spanish Colonial house where the artist lady lived.

As she had done several times before during this Lenten season, the artist lady came from her house as she heard the chanters approaching. She knew they would be coming because an hour earlier one Brother had gone through the village spinning the matraca, a wooden ratchet-type instrument that *alerted the villagers of the pending service. No bells were allowed to ring on Good Friday.*

She liked to stand in her garden just inside the wall as the Brothers passed. She knew many of them and without looking towards her, they would raise their voices a notch or two as they passed her gate because they knew she was there.

Adios acompañamiento	*Good-by all this company,*
Que me estuvieron velando	*Who have been here at my wake,*
Se me llego la hora y tiempo	*The hour and time have come*
De que me vallan sacando	*When you must take me out.*

Adios mis amados padres	*Good-by, my loving parents,*
Que conservádon mi vida,	*Who conserved my life,*
ya se lléga la hora y tiempo	*The hour and the time have come*
Ya se llegó mi partida.	*For me to take my parting.*

Normally she would return to her house after they passed, but this was Good Friday and the Brothers were on their way to Mass at Santo Tomás Church in the nearby village plaza.

"Come with me, Paul. Let's follow the Brothers to the Church."

Paul put down his tools and cleaned his hands, smoothed down his hair and tucked in his shirt, then walked with the lady out her gate and fell in behind the chanting Brothers.

As they neared the plaza they could hear other chanters coming from the opposite direction. These were the Brothers from the Moquí morada on the other side of the village. They were chanting the same alabado. At first it seemed as if the two groups were singing at odds against each other, creating a cacophony of sound, but as they began to merge in the center of the plaza, at the cross that had stood for years in front of the church, all 200 voices were in unison, each trying to out-chant the other as they raised their song in praise.

The Brothers entered the church, chanting as they went. Paul and the artist lady followed along with many other villagers who had lined the plaza to observe the Brothers' processional. The church was already full when they entered. As was the practice when the artist lady went to church, someone near her would make room for her to sit. Several people on the last bench moved so she could sit. Paul stood nearby.

Before the service concluded the artist lady would rise and signal to Paul that it was time to go. She always liked to leave these public events before they ended. This way she could avoid any unnecessary intrusion by people who may not know how she valued her privacy.

~ ~ ~ ~ ~ ~

Miss O'Keeffe would often ask me, or one of the other workers, to accompany her when she attended any of the public functions in our village. I think this made her feel more welcomed and accepted if she appeared with a villager. Plus, she liked us to be her shield or "body guards" if there were any intrusive tourists lurking about. By the time she had settled in our village she had become a well-known artist worldwide. I was well over 6' tall by the time I was 15 and broad shouldered, too. I think she liked me around as a buffer to the outside world.

She was interested in the *Pentitentes* and was impressed by the fact that these men devoted their time and effort to care for the people in the village. She had painted their crosses many times. Many of the men knew her and worked for her at one time or another. They would always show off as they chanted past her home and she would smile in recognition and appreciation.

Our main *morada, Morada de Nuestra Señora de Dolores del Alto,* had been in our village for over 400 years. The *Penitentes* or Brothers of the Light, have existed in New Mexico since the late 1790s. At the time when I accompanied Miss O'Keeffe to the Good Friday service there were over 200 Brothers in our village supporting two separate *moradas.*

Today there is only one active *morada*, *Morada del Alto* just up the road from the O'Keeffe home. The other *morada*, in the upper plaza of Abiquiú known as Moqui, is no longer active. Occasionally, Brothers from the *Morada del Alto* will go there to chant a Rosary or help maintain the structure, but for the most part the remaining Brothers in our village, which now number about 20, practice in *Morada del Alto*.

In the early days when Christianity was brought to these remote mountains, the priest could not possibly service the entire population. The Brothers became servants of the church as they performed Rosaries for the dead, prepared burial plots, helped grieving families, cared for widows and orphans and conducted many functions that would be similar to a church deacon today. Their organization is separate, but still a part of the Catholic Church.

St. Tomás the Apostle Catholic Church in Abiquiú has been the backdrop for many events in the Garcia family's life. Napoleón celebrated his first communion here soon after the church was built in 1937. Photo by Analinda

The Brothers were called upon to perform all functions of the Church, including weddings and baptisms. The Brothers were also the sole officiating clergy when New Spain became Mexico and Spain was no longer in control. There was a period before the expelled Spanish priests could be replaced with sanctioned priests provided by the Mexican leadership of the Catholic Church, and the Brothers filled the religious needs of the people.

For many the image of a Penitent is one who employs self flagellation and corporal punishment as part of paying penitence during these religious ceremonies. It is true that these practices were used in the past—and some say may still be performed in privacy; but the true mission of the Brothers is one of community service to fellow villagers.

When I was young I can remember a night during Holy Week when about half our village would walk down to Tierra

Morada del Alto *in Abiquiú commands one of the most beautiful views of the Chama River Valley. Napoleón is honored to be considered one of the Helpers for the Brothers of the Light, the* Pentitentes. *Photo by Analinda*

Azul, about 10 miles toward Española. They would carry the large *santos* from the *morada* and then perform a vigil throughout the night and walk back with the *santos* the next morning. On another night all the women would meet at the *morada* and then proceed up the hill to the cemetery *on their knees*. These practices have all fallen away. Membership in the Brothers has fallen, too, but those that remain are just as dedicated as were the earlier Brothers.

Today the Brothers meet once or twice a month in their *morada* to pray the Rosary. They still conduct the Rosary for a deceased member of the community and perform any other functions requested by the family of the deceased. Their main activities occur during the Lenten period, especially Holy Week. During this time the Brothers will spend many hours at prayer and will perform chanting processionals around

Napoleón Garcia at Santa Rosa de Lima Church ruins, the first church in Abiquiú, 2007. Photo by Analinda

the village and visiting the cemetery and church. They will also visit *moradas* in other villages and those Brothers would

Santa Rosa de Lima Church in Winter, 2007. Photo by Analinda

return the favor. There are women and men helpers who provide for the Brothers during this time of strict observance of prayer. The women helpers have a major role supporting the Brothers. They provide the food during Holy Week and help maintain the *morada* so that it presents a homelike atmosphere. Many of the Brothers' activities remain secret but all are in support of learning about the life of Christ and how best to emulate Christ's behavior in our modern world.

I became a helper to the Brothers about eight years ago after I lost my wife. I needed more support to help me with my grieving. My wife's death was very hard on our family because she was still so very young. She had been ill for a long time, but her passing was still a shock to us all.

To join the Brothers I had to go to them on my own volition. They do not recruit members. They accepted me and I was initiated as a helper. A helper supports the Brothers in any of their functions. Don't even ask me about their secret functions because that is one area in which I am not allowed to participate. I have always respected the Brotherhood of the *Penitentes* and have seen the results of their good deeds in my village. I enjoy the prayers and chanting the *alabados* and feel very fortunate to be among their number.

One event in which I participated was a special service for a man in Santa Fe. He was not a Brother but had always supported and respected the organization. As he neared death he asked his family to invite the Brothers from all the nearby villages to come and perform a service for him. I went with the Brothers from Abiquiú to chant this service in the St. Francis Cathedral of Santa Fe. Brothers from other villages such as El Rito, Truchas, Chimayó, and Cordova also were in attendance. There were about 75 Brothers in all. The coffin was in the front of the altar and all the participating Brothers filed down the aisle and circled the coffin several times chanting and praying. We then proceeded to the back of the Cathedral and continued with our chants. It was a very moving experience, not only for us but for every person in attendance.

Recently a group of Lutheran pastors visited me to learn more about my connection with the Brothers. They were attending a retreat at the Ghost Ranch. The pastors came from all over northern New Mexico and some from Colorado. Included was the Luthern Bishop of the New Mexico, Colorado and Utah Diocese. About 15 pastors squeezed onto my small front porch to ask questions about the Brothers and other items of interest about our village. The lead Brother of our *Morada del Alto* opened the sanctuary for the visiting clergy and gave a brief history of the organization and answered many questions. The pastors were deeply moved by this experience and expressed their appreciation over and

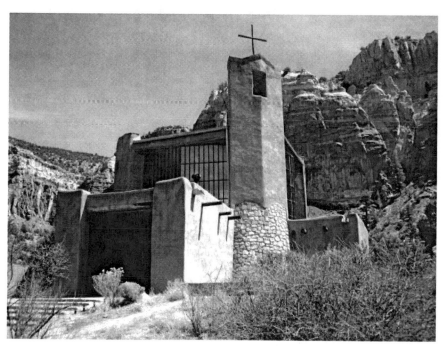

Napoelón's father-in-law, Joe Ferran, and several of his sons constructed the Christ in the Desert Monastery Church. The church is designed to blend in with the rocky cliff background. Photo by Analinda

over. Sharing the knowledge about the Brothers is another important function of this *Pentitente* organization.

Abiquiú Adobe, 2006. Photo by Analinda

Being *Genízaro*

Paul had just woken up on a Saturday morning. He had a long do-list of chores around his home. He was employed by one of the contractors associated with the Los Alamos National Lab. Each day he drove the 90 mile round trip up to the lab on the Parajito Mesa. On the weekends he tried to work on his ever-expanding house in order to house his ever-expanding family. However, this morning it was not meant to be. Soon after he had his first cup of coffee there was a knock at the door. There stood the artist lady for whom he occasionally chauffeured.

"Paul, I would like you to drive my friend and me up into the mountains behind the village. I want to show her the spring and the view from atop the Abiquiú Mesa."

Of course Paul agreed to the request because any extra money would certainly help his family. A little later he walked the short distance from his home to the home of the artist. The old white Volkswagon van was waiting in the driveway and he could hear the women inside getting ready for their outing. He waited by the car until they came out, carrying their lunch pack and blankets. It was a mild summer day and he thought that it would be a perfect day for such a trip.

The ladies climbed into the back seat as Paul slipped behind the wheel. He started the car and began the trip across the plaza, past the church, then turned left up a narrow road that led up to the mountains. He could see the white-knuckled, city-slicker visitor from New York gripping the door handle as if at any moment she would bolt from the bouncing car.

The road dipped down and crossed a shallow creek, then began to climb up into the mountains. They passed what seemed to be a rock wall on the left that bordered the edge of the road. It was not a wall, but a pile of carefully laid stones.

"Let's stop here for a minute," requested the artist lady.

She climbed out of the car and found a flat stone and fit it into the wall with the expertise of a native pueblo builder. Her friend, taking a deep breath from the brief break from the bouncing ride, watched with puzzlement.

"At this spot Indians massacred Spanish pioneers here in the early 19ᵗʰ century. It has become a tradition to place a stone as a memorial to these brave early settlers," explained the artist lady. Paul said a silent prayer for his ancestors—on both sides of the skirmish.

Her friend accepted this bit of historical knowledge without comment or participation in the ritual. After the lady returned to the car. Paul continued up the narrow road past the village water tower on the right. The artist lady had been very instrumental in getting water piped from the mountain spring into the village homes. Abiquiú was one of the first villages in northern New Mexico to have running water in their homes.

Soon they were following the creek up the narrow canyon. They could see the acequia *on the far left side that carried the irrigation water to the village gardens. The cottonwoods that outlined the path of the creek were in their full green splendor of summer. The cedar and piñon trees gave off enticing scents in the warm sunshine.*

They bounced across the creek several times. Paul would carefully approach the shallow waters, trying to avoid the rocks and sinkholes. He was very aware of the visitor from New York, sitting stiffly in the back seat with her death grip on the door handle.

"Take it easy, Paul, slow down and take these bumps a little slower," the artist lady commented.

Around a bend they encountered several cows on the side of the road. They lifted their heads momentarily, just long enough to acknowledge the presence of the humans.

"Who takes care of these cows way up here?" asked the New York visitor.

"Nobody takes care of them. They take care of themselves. Ranchers might come up occasionally to check on them, but for the most part they are on their own," Paul responded, thinking that the question had been directed at him.

The New Yorker was only familiar with the farming techniques of rural New York where cattle could not roam anywhere on there own.

Napoleón placing a rock at the Las Crucitas de Animas descanso that marks the spot in Abiquiú where early Spanish settlers were massacred by raiding Indians. Napoleón is honoring both his Spanish and Indian ancestors. Photo by Analinda

Soon they came to an area where the spring came down the mountains from two sources, meeting to form the one main creek that continued on down to the village. Paul pulled into an open space and parked the car. The women got out and began walking up one side of the creek.

Paul leaned against the car and took in the beauty of this very special place. This spot had meant so much to his ancestors for here was the source of life for his village—water. Paul recalled playing here as a young boy and having picnics with his family on the grassy banks. The creek was a source of watercress that he had picked and eaten all his life. He noticed that the women had come prepared with some containers, and the artist lady was showing her friend how to harvest the greens from the water, which was icy cold even in summer. Her friend had found a large boulder on which to lean and seemed rooted to that spot.

Up the left bank of the creek Paul noticed some movement in the water. Slowly and with great stealth, he walked around the boulders that line the creek and approached the pool of water from its deep end. He had seen a large fish circling in the pool. His shadow and slow movements in the water forced the fish toward the shallow end of the pool. When the fish sensed its predator it began to make a dash back into the deeper end but Paul was ready. With one swift movement he leaned over and scooped the fish into his hands as it tried to dart back to the safety of the deeper water. Paul tossed the fish over onto the bank.

He looked up and saw the women staring in disbelief at what they had just seen.

"Paul, how did you catch that fish like that? I see all these men up on the river, fishing all day without catching a thing; and here you scoop down and catch one with your bare hands!" exclaimed the artist lady.

"I've done this all my life," replied Paul. "This is where I've played since I was a kid and we would always trap and catch

fish here in this narrow creek with its deep pools.

Paul returned the fish to the water. To Paul it was just another expression of his native heritage. He was proud of being Genízaro. His Native American ancestors would have been proud of him this day.

The women climbed back into the car and Paul continued to drive them on up onto the mesa that overlooked the land of the Abiquiú Grant. As the women walked among the piñon trees, Paul walked over to the edge of the mesa and took in the view of his ancestral lands. Even though he had lived a poor existence on this land and he continued to struggle to feed and care for his family, his heart and soul filled with pride as he sensed the history that was unfolding in front of him. He was proud to a Genízaro. He was proud to think his ancestors had cared for this land and it was still here and would provide for Paul and his descendants for years to come.

෴ ෴ ෴ ෴ ෴ ෴

Not a day goes by without my having to explain what being a *Genízaro* means. In the early days, when the Spanish were in control of this region, there was a great need of laborers for the large Spanish ranches. The Spanish colonists participated in the very active slave trade provided by the roving bands of Plains Indians. They would either buy or capture youths of various nomadic tribes that roamed the mountains of northern New Mexico. These captives would be baptized and given Christian names. They grew up in the Hispanic culture and soon forgot much of their native ways. When they reached maturity they were given their freedom; however, most of them would stay right where they were because by this time this was their home and many would have already married and started families.

Each time I try to explain being *Genízaro* I am asked "from which tribe was my family taken." The act of being baptized and given Christian names was to deliberately erase any reference to prior "heathen" or "savage" connections. Along with the Christianization came the strict lessons of the Catholic Church that were intended to remove any practice of non-Christian rituals. History has shown that the *Genízaro* came from many of the nomadic tribes, such as the Navajo, Utes, Comanches, Kiowa, Pawnee, Apache, and other non-Pueblo Indians that roamed in this area at the time of the early Spanish colonization.

Lesley Poling-Kemper defines the origin of the word *Genízaro* in her book, *Valley of Shining Stone, The Story of Abiquiú,* as follows: "The word *genízaro* is derived from the Turkish *yeniceri* or *yenicheri*—*yeni,* new, and *cheri,* troops." Turkish military brought the term to Spain and thus to the New World. However, the term was purely an ethnic designation with no military connotations when it was used in New Mexico. *Genízaro* is sometimes mistakenly used to described people who were half-breed. But our original *Genízaro* are completely Native American. The subsequent generations did intermarry with the Spaniards in this area.

Another strategic reason for the Spanish to create a *Genízaro* population was for defense purposes. The Spanish found it increasingly difficult to protect the Spanish ranchers in the outlying areas around Santa Fe. The *Genízaro* increased the population that would be favorable to the Spanish investments in these remote regions. Groups of *Genízaro* are found in other areas of northern New Mexico, but our village of Abiquiú is the most well-known *Genízaro* settlement.

The village of Abiquiú had been settled and abandoned several times due to the raiding activities of the Plains Indians in this remote section of northern New Mexico. In 1754, Thomas Velez Capuchin, the Spanish governor at that time, officiated a land grant to a group of *Genízaro* in the Abiquiú area. This is what is known as the Abiquiú Land Grant, consisting of 16,000 acres, and is the only Spanish Land Grant given to *Genízaro,* or to persons of non-Spanish ancestry.

Governor Capuchin was noted for his fairness with and understanding of the native population in this area. The *Genízaro* appreciated the compassion expressed by the governor. Perhaps this compassionate treatment shown the *Genízaro* at the time of the Land Grant created the enduring pride my people have shown for their land, even up until present day. This compassion for native peoples had not been the case with earlier Spanish administrators or those who would follow Capuchin. The pride in their grant has been carried forward throughout the *Genízaro* descendents. When greedy land grabbers overran this area, the *Genízaro* in Abiquiú have successfully fought and retained their property rights. One instance of potential loss of land occurred in the 1920s when Abiquiú was given the choice of becoming a recognized pueblo or a village in the state of New Mexico. The people in Abiquiú had seen the destitute living conditions in some of the neighboring pueblos so they elected to become a village. Along with this designation came the requirement to pay taxes. The *Genízaro* in Abiquiú entrusted their tax payments with an individual who failed to use the funds properly. They nearly lost their lands by defaulting on their taxes. They successfully fought and won their land back.

In 1821, when Mexico took control of New Spain and the Spanish rule ended, the term *Genízaro* was no longer used because the practice of capturing and enslaving young Plains Indians ceased when the Spanish left. All pueblo inhabitants were given full citizenship rights. However, the term does still exist among those of us who have kept the pride of our ancestors alive and have tried to hand this knowledge down to our children so that they will know and appreciate who they are and what their ancestors have done for them.

Miss O'Keeffe was always amazed when she would discover some of our native ways of doing things. The story of my catching the fish with my bare hand is but one example when she stood speechless as she discovered yet another insight into who we were. She often expressed her delight in discovering our traditional ways and constantly insisted that she had no desire to change any of the things we did, but she was inquisitive in why we did things the way we did. She couldn't understand why the women always did the plastering of the pueblos. The small, delicate hands of the women would become red and raw from the gritty clay and swollen from being in the water all day. The men might be the ones to get and mix the heavy clay, but the women did the detail work. The only answer I had for her was, "We have always done it this way." There are many Native American tribes where the women build and "own" the homes. Perhaps this has been carried into our traditional ways of living, also.

I am reminded of another time my *Genízaro* ways amazed Miss O'Keeffe and her guests. I was working at her home one day and while passing through the courtyard she came to the door and said, "Paul, come quick. There is a spider on the wall here!"

I walked into the house, found the offending spider, scooped it up in my gloved hands and took it outside. The guests were speechless when they saw how I removed the spider without so much as a display of fear or concern. I suppose they thought I'd swat it, spray it, get a gun and shoot it, or however else these city folks could imagine ridding themselves of invading monsters. It was always amusing to me to see how these folks tried to adjust to country living. Miss O'Keeffe always stood in wonder at these displays and would smile briefly to herself in the realization that she was witnessing yet another aspect of *Genízaro* skills.

When the Spaniards created the *Genízaro* population it was their initial intent to erase all affiliation with prior tribal customs; however, they could not remove the deep-seated culture implanted by our ancestors. We still have our annual Indian Fiesta each November. For two days we all become

Indians. We dance, we eat, but we also attend a special Mass and end the festivities with a Rosary in honor of our ancestors.

They couldn't erase our need for the *curanderas*, either. There never were enough doctors to care for the needs of our people. *Curanderas* would practice their ancient healing using herbs and mysterious potions that would cure many ailments. Many *Genízaro* children were delivered by the midwife curanderas.

The practices of the *curanderas* did cause some problems in the mid 19th century because some of these practices were investigated as being withcraft. This led to many trials that have been recorded in legal documents and books written by academics who attempted to determine if indeed there were witches in Abiquiú. I believe that there were no witches practicing in Abiquiú. The ancient healing practices of our *curanderas* were grossly misinterpreted.

We have always relied on our native plants to supplement our food supply. I know that pioneers who settled all over our country had to rely on many of these same self-reliance skills, but our people continue their use even today. We still gather the watercress from the spring, and search for green *verdolagas* along the banks of creeks in summer. Some of the wild plants that we still seek for our use are: *chimajá*, the very first green to appear in the spring; *quelites*, a wild spinach; *guaco*, a tall, skinny plant very much like spinach; *cebolla*, a wild onion; *yerba buena*, spearmint; *poleó*, peppermint; the long root of the wild white radish is used like we use carrots today; asparagus can be found growing alongside the streams and ditches; *piñon*, pine nuts, are a delicacy we can only harvest every three or four years; and there are many varieties of berries that we eat right from the tree or bushes or dry for later use. These plants can be used year around because many of them can be dried for use in winter. Just the other day my cousin gave me a small bag of *ocha* root. The root of the *ocha* is used as a mouth rinse for internal infections or used as a balm externally. I understand that if you put some in your pocket this will ward off rattlesnakes.

I've even seen some of our *Genízaro* cows stand for hours licking the side of our cliffs in order to get some salt into their diet. However, I don't recall any people getting salt in this way.

I have a lot of fun "being *Genízaro*". I use it to explain many of my shortcut methods of fixing things. I'm famous for my over-use of silver duct tape as the main material for repairs. I call it "*Genízaro* solder". A friend of mine broke her watchband. As an expedient measure she tied her watch around her neck using a shoestring. I had to compliment her on her nice "*Genízaro* watch".

The Family

*Paul was in the kitchen surrounded by his young family.
His wife, Emma, was busy making* tortillas *and trying to keep
greedy little hands from swiping them as soon as they came off*

*Napoleón Garcia with his three daughters, Rebecca, Marie and Grace, 2007.
Photo by Analinda*

the stove.

"Stop that! If you keep it up there will be no tortillas *left for dinner," said the frustrated Mother.*

Napoleón and Emma Garcia with their three youngest children, Dominic, Rebecca, and Marie. Garcia Family Photo

Paul was no help since his hand was one of the fastest in grabbing the hot, fresh tortillas.

"Grace, go see who that is. If we know them, invite them in," said Paul to his oldest child in response to a knock at the front door.

Grace soon returned, followed by the artist lady who lived just around the corner. It was the habit of the artist to visit some of the families that lived in the village. She was especially fond of Paul's family for Paul had worked for her since he himself was a child. Paul and Emma immediately began to tidy the kitchen and make room for the lady to sit.

"It was such a beautiful fall day that I just could not stay inside," remarked the artist lady. "I was walking around the

"Pancho Villa and His Gang" — Napoleón Garcia and his seven sons, Theadore, Napoleón Jr. (Nappy), Leo, Antonio. Napoleón Sr., Dennis, Howard, and Dominic with his son Andres, 2001. Garcia Family Photo

plaza when I realized that I had not seen your family for a while, Paul. How are...." It was then that the artist lady noticed that Emma was wearing a smock covering her bulging stomach. "Emma, are you pregnant again!?" she exclaimed, with great emphasis on the word again.

Embarrassed, but smiling, Emma confirmed the fact that she indeed was expecting their fifth child.

"Paul, how in the world are you going to be able to support such a large family?" the artist lady asked.

Cousin Roland Fernandez, Grandmother Lucia Suazo, Napoleón and Emma Garcia with three youngest children, Dominic, Marie, and Rebecca. Garcia Family Photo

Napoleón Garcia, 2004. Garcia Family Photo

Napoleón's oldest son, Leo, has become a successful woodcarving artist. He has his gallery, Galeria de Don Cachuate, off the Abiquiú Plaza just around the corner from his Dad's gallery. He shares his gallery with his partner, Barbara Manzanares, who is a recognized weaver on the Fabric Arts Trail in New Mexico. Photo by Analinda

"God will provide," was Paul's short answer. He was not as gracious as his wife had been to this impolite inquiry.

Just at that time Leo ran into the room. The artist lady had taken a strong liking to Paul's oldest son. Leo was bubbling over with the news from school about the movie that was being filmed there and HE was going to be in it! He wanted to share this news with his friend the artist.

"They came in with their big cameras and microphones. They even had to bring in their own lights! We had to sit at our desks and act like we were very busy. Then they followed us outside to recess and we had to play the same game over and over again until they said we got it right. I'm going to be in the movies!" exclaimed the third grader.

A film company had come to Abiquiú to film the award-winning children's story, And Now Miguel. Some of the school

Napoleón taught Leo all he knew about woodcarving and is very proud to see him take it even further, producing santos *and* retablos *that have found their way into many collectors' homes, Photo by Analinda*

scenes were being filmed at the small village school that Paul's children attended. The village had been all abuzz with the excitement of Hollywood stars in their midst.

The artist lady had long been interested in this young man and had shown concern when she learned that Leo was having some difficulties with reading in school. She knew of a special reading tutor and had made the arrangements for Leo to obtain help with his reading.

"Leo, do you have the book that the movie is based on?" asked the lady.

"Yes. I'll get it to show you," answered the boy.

"How is he doing with his reading lessons?" asked the lady when the boy had scurried from the room.

"We'll let you find out for yourself," said Paul as Leo returned with the book.

Leo leaned against the small lady as he opened the book and proudly began to read the story to her—fluently.

∾ ∾ ∾ ∾ ∾ ∾

Miss O'Keeffe would often visit the families in the village. She particularly liked the families with children. It has been said that she got along better with children than she did with adults. However, she never could hide her amazement as she watched our families grow. She did take an interest in my children, especially Leo. He used to go with me when I worked at her house. He grew up very fast and was soon taller than me. Without her help he would never had made it through school. If he had passed through elementary school without learning to read he would have lost interest and fallen behind his classmates. Our little village school just didn't have the resources to give him the extra help that he needed. But Miss O'Keeffe stepped in and paid for a tutor in Santa Fe where we would take him once a week for lessons. Soon he was able to succeed in reading. Just as Miss O'Keeffe had done for my brother Jackie, she recognized Leo's artistic talent and encouraged him to paint. Of all my children Leo has the most artistic talent and today has his own gallery here in the village. I taught him to carve, but he very soon surpassed me. He also paints *retablos* and murals. His specialty in woodcarving is *santos*; St. Francis is his most popular one.

Family has always been very important to me. I have tried with my own family to fill the voids I faced growing up without having a supportive family. Of course I could never had accomplished this without having the perfect partner, my wife, Emma.

Emma Rose Ferran was the daughter of a respectable family. Her grandfather had come from France and was a landowner in the El Rito area. Her father was a respected community leader and building contractor in Abiquiú. Emma and I began meeting at the village church on Sundays. When I had an extra nickel I would buy her a Coke at the

On a trip to Chicago, Napoleón finally got to see the huge painting, Above the Clouds, at the Art Institute of Chicago. He had only seen glimpse of this massive painting through the garage door at O'Keeffe's Ghost Ranch home and was glad to finally see this "mysterious" painting that was kept from curious eyes while it was being produced. Garcia Family Photo.

village store. There weren't many extra nickels at that time because I was helping my mother buy a small adobe house in the settlement called Moque above the village.

I don't know what Emma saw in me, but she was determined to marry me. I just thank God I found her. I

The proud father, Napoleón, with his two youngest children, Marie and Rebecca, at their First Communion. Garcia Family Photo.

often wondered why did she care? Why did she pay attention to me? But despite her family's reservations we were married in 1950 when I was 19 and Emma was 16.

Grace was born in 1951 while we were living in two rooms I had added to my mother's house. Leo and Teddie were born in Utah where I had gone to work at the Army Depot. We were in Utah for five years. After the end of the Korean Conflict we returned to Abiquiú. Emma's father, now reconciled to me, helped us acquire a small three-room adobe on the plaza here in Abiquiú. Those three rooms became the heart of the big house that you see now where I raised my family and where I still live.

I was present at the birth of all of my children except Howard. I was working in Cuba, New Mexico at that time. My father-in-law took my wife to the hospital and Howard was born before I could get there. Dennis gave us the most concern when he was born. I was working in Los Alamos. I took my wife to the hospital, but then I had to go to work after the baby was born. I soon got a phone call to come back to the hospital right away. The baby was having trouble swallowing and if he couldn't swallow he would die. I had to take him to the children's hospital in Denver. The hospital made plane arrangements and we flew to Denver. They didn't even let my wife see Dennis in the hospital before we left for Denver. After seven days the staff in Denver were successful in getting him to swallow. They believed that the nurses in Española had tried to force him to swallow, causing him to shut down the swallowing reflex, and that may have caused some damage. My wife came on home to Abiquiú while I was in Denver. So, when I took him home seven days later it was the first time she saw him. The reason I tell of these births is because my children are such an important part of my life. Their entry into my life was always a life-changing event for me.

All of my children finished high school. For some it was

easy, for others we had to struggle. After high school three went to college, others attended community colleges or trade schools, and several completed tours of military service. We were able to live in Santa Fe for five years so that our older children could attend St. Michaels High School; but finances dictated that we return to Abiquiú. My children are all employed in a variety of endeavors from surveying, electronics, nursing, clerical, home building and caring for the disabled. All have married except Dennis and I now have 21 grandchildren and 16 great-grandchildren that keep me busy.

Our first child was a girl, and then we had seven boys and finished up with two more girls. When the last two girls came along I told my wife that I had been putting up with the boys with all their sports and carting them around. These two are yours, I told her. *You* get to take them around to all their sports. Of course that didn't happen. I was still there for them, too.

I am very proud of my children. It makes my heart glad to know that they are so close and care for each other as they do. They fight and squabble like most brothers and sisters but they are always there for each other when needed. I grew up without the support of family, so the one thing I taught my kids was to respect each other. In this I can see that I succeeded, and that makes me very happy.

I'm still raising these ten children and their children and their children's children! Not a day goes by without some one of them needing something, and they know they can come to me. Some don't have phones, so my house is their phone booth and I sometimes act as their secretary taking and delivering messages. Several times a week one of them needs to borrow my car for some reason or another—always a good reason, of course. My children know they can drop in for a meal or collect food from the pantry any time...and of course there is always the need to borrow a little cash—just to get by. I grew up without a supportive family so I know how important it is to have one. It is my life's mission to care and support my family in any way that I am physically and financially able. However, these late night calls to come for someone who has run out of gas or has a flat tire are getting harder to deal with as I get older!

With Miss O'Keeffe's help, I had purchased four acres of land here in Abiquiú, bordering the creek. I was driving for her one day when she pointed out this piece of land to me. She said she knew the owner who lived in New York. "Why don't you buy that land, Paul?" she said to me. I thought it was a great idea. She contacted her friend and soon the deal was struck and we owned the property. Our plan was to build a home there, but our children came too fast and too many. We just kept adding on to the home we had in the village.

I had the land partitioned into ten lots and gave each kid their own lot. They are all building homes there except Rebecca, who has her own home, and Grace, who sold her lot to Howard because she wanted to live in El Rito. Howard has a cabin on his lot, but he lives in Santa Fe. Leo has a home there—actually it is the original home that came with the land, but he is living in his Grandpa Ferran's home and hopes to be able to buy it some day. He is also buying land in El Rito. He will probably sell his lot to one of the other kids some day. The kids who live there get along fine and enjoy being neighbors. They are all very close and look out for each other. All my children live within the vicinity of Abiquiú, except Howard, but he spends many weekends here.

I was hired as a laborer at the Los Alamos National Lab and made foreman soon afterward in spite of my sketchy education. I retired in 1993 after working there for 35 years. We raised ten kids on a laborer's wages. Most of the time, I just gave my check to my wife and she managed everything. She might give me a little out of it after she cashed it. She knew I couldn't be trusted with money. I never gambled or drank it away, but I would hand money to children and teens who looked hungry, or needed shoes. Over the past seven years I have been going with my church to Nicaragua as a missionary. Seeing the hungry kids there breaks my heart. I will always hand out all the money I take and will share whatever food I have with them if it is possible.

My wife developed diabetes and died at age 65. Before she grew too ill, we took a trip to Europe. We landed in Madrid, Spain, and then went to all those places in Europe—Venice, Paris, Switzerland. She's been dead for eight years now and I think I'm still paying for that trip, but it was worth it. I have such happy memories. It has been hard for me since her death. Although our children were grown, we were still very involved with our large family, and I try to continue that still. I wish she were still here to help me with the children, especially the grandchildren and great-grandchildren.

After my wife's death, I increased my interest in

Chimney Rock—landscape seen from Ghost Ranch—subject of several Georgia O'Keeffe paintings, 2006 . Photo by Analinda

woodcarving. I set up a small gallery on my front porch where I could work and display the crosses and miniature Kiva ladders that I carve from aspen. Gradually I noticed that I was becoming a tourist attraction myself. People visiting my village would knock on my door and ask questions. I answered them as best I could. I told them where to find the old pueblo ruins and where to go to see what O'Keeffe saw. I have maps of the scenic routes through the surrounding country. I sometimes lead small groups to points of local interest, and will talk at length about the history and folklore of the area. The tourist population is increasing as interest in O'Keeffe's work increases, and people travel great distances to see the country that inspired so many of her paintings. This is my country, too, and I enjoy sharing it with visitors who express an interest.

I share my home with two cockatiels and I have over 50 homing pigeons out back that live in a pen with two chickens,

Lavender Hills between Abiquiú and Ghost Ranch—subject of several Georgia O'Keeffe paintings, 2006 Photo by Analinda

a rooster and a hen. Feeding and caring for my birds offers a great deal of relaxation for me. I dabble a little bit in my garden, weather permitting and we have enough rain. Although I live alone, my house is still full of life and living.

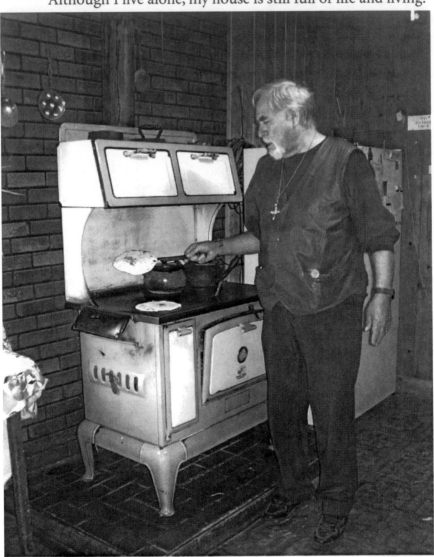

The wood stove in Napoleon's kitchen used to belong to Georgia O'Keeffe. In addition to warming his home on cold winter mornings it makes excellent tortillas. Photo by Analinda

Epilogue

I continued to work for Miss O'Keeffe, off and on, even while working full-time in Los Alamos. She would still come to my door and request me to drive her to events or to run errands. Her interactions with the village ended in the early 1970s when Juan Hamilton began to manage her affairs. She was in her late 80s at this time and was already nearly blind. With Juan as her companion she began to travel all over the world, so she was not at home in Abiquiú very much. In 1984, when she became ill, Juan moved her into Santa Fe where she could be closer to medical care. She died in 1986 at the age of 99.

I know that the part I shared is only a small portion of her long, productive life; however, knowing and working for her was a great experience for my family and me. I always appreciated the fact that she accepted me as I was, just like she accepted our villagers' way of life. I felt that she understood and trusted me because no one else ever did. On cold winter mornings I build a fire in the old wood stove that used to be in her kitchen but now warms my home.

Abiquiú Elder

In March of 2004 *The Albuquerque Journal* wrote a feature article about me and referred to me as an Abiquiú Elder. I guess that now that I'm 76 I should not be offended by that title. I'm just glad to still be here!

After I retired in 1993 I returned to my hobby of woodcarving. I like to carve crosses, Kiva ladders, walking sticks, and *retablos*. I turned my front porch into a gallery for my woodcarving. Tourists began coming to my door and asking questions about O'Keeffe, the village and the area in general. I soon found myself in the tourist business, offering guided tours to the nearby sights.

Often the tourist would ask me if I knew any stories about the area. I love to tell stories. Storytelling is an age-old tradition in my culture. Here are some of the stories that I

Napoleón Garcia at work in his woodcarving studio, 2007. Photo by Analinda

have told over the years to my children and to the tourists who come onto my porch seeking a closer look into what makes Abiquiú "Abiquiú".

My Ghosts

Here in my own home, my wife, children and I have all witnessed strange happenings. I would say that we definitely have a spirit or ghost that dwells within our home. When we are in our beds, sometimes we will get the feeling that someone is in the room with us. Although we can see that no one is actually in the room, there is a strong sensation of a presence. Very soon after we have this feeling, the spirit will make its presence known to us by loud footsteps walking up and down the stairs. The sound of the footsteps will enter our bedrooms, and our mattresses will actually show the indentation of a body sitting at the foot of the bed! At first I might think that it is one of the family who has entered the room. But when I turn to look I see that there is no one there. We all hear these footsteps walking from room to room. We believe that the ghost is the spirit of a man because of the heavy, loud footsteps.

The ghost also moves such items as my woodcarving tools and coffee cups filled with freshly poured hot coffee! I will look all about the house for these items, and they are nowhere to be found. People will say that I'm just being forgetful and forget where I put these things. However, I eventually discover these items in rooms where they do not belong, nor does it make any sense for their being there. I think that the ghost is a friendly spirit because if it wanted to do us any harm, he would have done so a long time ago. I think he just wants to play and visit with us.

Sometimes when it is very quiet, like in the early morning or during the night, I hear knocking as if someone were at the door to my room. More than once I have answered the door and found that there is no one there. During the day, I don't notice it as much because I'm up and moving around and other noises would cover up the knocking. However, I've gone to the door during the day thinking a tourist has arrived to find no tourist either at the front, side or back doors.

La Llorona

The people of the village also tell of a woman who is heard screaming or crying. The sound comes from the cemetery that is located up above the village, just west of the *Morada del Alto*. This woman is dressed in dark clothing, and allows people to view her only from a distance. When anyone attempts to get close to her, she disappears. I have heard about this woman for many years. For lack of a better word to describe her, we all just refer to her as *La Llorona*, the weeping woman.

The story of *La Llorona* as told in Abiquiú is about a man in the village who was very mean and abusive to his wife. They had two children, a boy and girl. One day he came home drunk and beat her until she became unconscious. When she awoke she found that her husband and two children were gone. From that day on this mother has been hunting for her children. She continues to search for them, crying and calling for her children.

The legend of *La Llorona* is one of the oldest stories in the Southwest. It has survived in Spanish folklore for over four centuries. The version most New Mexicans are familiar with comes from Mexico and Bolivia. The legend tells of a love affair between a peasant girl and a rich man who refuses to marry her. She gives birth to two of his children and later murders them in despair, or for revenge, or to keep them away from their father and his family. After her conviction and execution for their murders, she haunts the waterways near the villages and towns searching for her lost children.

The story told in Abiquiú does not tell of her killing her own children. I like our version much better. Some mothers use this story to keep their kids close to home, telling them that if they hear or see *La Llorona* she will take them away thinking that they are her lost children.

Witches

I can remember that as a young boy, I would see balls of light bouncing off the roofs of houses in the village. My friends and I would sit on a bench in the plaza at night, and we would witness these strange lights, becoming quite scared. Our parents would tell us that the lights were witches, so we were very cautious and afraid. This kept us close to home, which was probably why our parents told us that the lights were witches.

One quite well-known story is of a witch that lived in the village many years ago. The people feared this woman and left her alone. Because of her powers she was known to have the ability to turn herself into animal forms. This transformation allowed her to sneak up to houses and peer into windows without drawing the attention of the occupants. By doing this, she used the information she gathered against people to either harm them or bribe them to get what she wanted.

One evening, an unusually large black owl kept flying around the village. The people suspected that it was the witch who had transformed herself into an owl. The people believed her to be evil, so they approached a man and asked him to kill the owl. The man brought out his rifle. Before he placed the bullets in the chamber, he took out his pocketknife and carved a cross on the tips. It was believed that by marking the tips with a cross would ensure that the bullet would reach its mark and kill the witch.

The man went to where the owl had been spotted, took aim, and fired. The bullet hit the owl and in a cloud of black feathers, the owl flew away into the nearby hills. The following day the old woman, whom the people suspected to be the witch, was seen in her yard with a large, bloodied bandage wrapped around her shoulder. A coincidence? What do you think?

In Robert Julyan's book *The Place Names of New Mexico*, he states that some people suggest the name Abiquiú originated from *Abechiu,* which is said to mean "hooting owl". I wonder if this has anything to do with this story about the Owl Witch?

In the late 18th century, the Catholic Church instigated several witch trials in Abiquiú that have been documented in legal papers and have appeared in many publications about Abiquiú. However, I feel that this is just a misinterpretation of some of our ancient practices used by the *curanderas.* *Curanderas* were people, either men or women, who have extensive knowledge of using plants and herbs for healing and curing the people. I think that it is highly probable that the locals were upset about restrictions imposed on their practices by the Catholic Church. They just might have used some of these potions against the people who were trying to change and disrupt their ancient ways of doing things.

Some stories concerning witchcraft practices involved the age-old love triangle. A wife might seek out the skills of a *curandera* to get a potion to harm her husband if he was suspected of cheating on his wife or perhaps she would seek a potion to make him love her, and only her. I'm not saying that it was always the wife! But it usually involved some member of a love triangle. *Curanderas* also would remove bullets or arrows resulting from battles. They had the surgical skill that today we see in doctors. But then it was seen as a miracle if they could heal a warrior who had been considered mortally wounded.

I think I have inherited healing powers from my ancestors. There have been many times I have been able to use my hands in alleviating aches and pains experienced by my family and friends. When I was working my co-workers would seek me out if they had a pain in a joint or even a joint out of place. I could place my hands, and with the help of a silent prayer, the joint would be relieved. I like to think that God was using me to help the healing process. Another type of healing I think I assisted was getting sick people to eat. For example, when both my mother and later my wife were ill, and could not eat, they would call me to eat with them because there was something about the way I ate that would make them hungry and their appetites would return. I have been told that I treat food as if it were my art medium. Some artists work in oils and watercolor as I work with food.

Ghost Ranch ... Ever wonder how it got its name?

Ghost Ranch is located about 15 miles north of Abiquiú. It was once one of the largest Spanish Land Grants in this area. In the 20th century, it became famous as a dude ranch that attracted many Easterners to the wild, wild, West. Georgia O'Keeffe was one of these Easterners. She first went to Ghost Ranch, where she bought a house before settling in Abiquiú. Ghost Ranch now is owned by the Presbyterian Church and is used for religious retreats and cultural workshops. Years ago Ghost Ranch was called *Rancho de los Brujos,* or Ranch of the Witches. Cattle rustlers used to steal cattle from the local ranchers and take them into a box canyon at *Rancho de los Brujos*. If anyone dared to be so brave as to follow these phantom rustlers into the canyon, they would never be seen again! Stories are told of ghostly sounds of horses, gunfights, and balls of fire that bounce off the canyon walls. Balls of light or fire were considered evidence that witches were nearby. The designation of witches was changed over the years to ghosts because of the phantom-type occurrences that were reported.

There are stories that tell about travelers who were enticed to spend the night in this area only to be never seen again nor would there be any trace of their existence. However, some of their belongings would appear with the family that lived nearby.

The Mysterious *Penitente*

There is a story that people tell in the village. Now I have heard this story since I was just a small boy. The story is about a member of the religious *penitente* brotherhood. Years ago the *penitentes* used to walk the dirt streets of the village on special religious holidays. They would wear a large handkerchief over their heads to disguise their identities. As they would walk the streets, some would carry a whip of knotted cords, which they used to self-flagellate themselves. They would do this to show their spiritual devotion and reverence to their Catholic religion.

There was one *penitente* who was different from the rest. This *penitente* would conduct his walk by himself at night. As he would make his way through the village, the people would show him respect by making the sign of the cross as he passed. The people did not recognize this strange devotee, but because of his strong self-sacrifice, they gave him respect nonetheless. This *penitente* also had an unusual habit of walking down roads that led away from the *morada*. When some individuals followed him at a distance, to their surprise, they discovered that he would simply disappear! Of course the village people knew immediately that this was no ordinary *penitente*, but a spiritual being.

As I have heard the story, there was one individual who decided to follow the *penitente* the next time he walked through the village. This young man wanted to prove to everyone that he was not afraid and was braver than the rest. He wanted to find out who this *penitente* was. The next time the *penitente* walked through the village, he was ready.

The night was very dark, and sure enough, the *penitente* walked by with the young man following behind. Nearing the edge of the village, the *penitente* noticed that he was being followed and extended his arm, gesturing for the young man to stop! He did not say anything; he just made it clear to him that he was not welcome to follow the *penitente* any further. The young man chose to disregard the warning and continued to follow.

The *penitiente* continued his walk, but this time he took a new route that led up to the cemetery. With the young man following close behind, they both entered the cemetery grounds. Well into the cemetery, the *penitente* slowed his pace, allowing the young man to get fairly close to him. When he got close enough to the *penitente*, the *penitente* stopped and turned to face the man. The young man walked right up to the *penitente* and asked, "Who are you?" Slowly the *penitiente* raised one arm to his head and took hold of the handkerchief. He then quickly pulled it off, reveling a white skull! Had the *penitiente* led the young man to his own grave? Was the mysterious penitente Death?

Free Range

Free Range means that livestock can range and take care of themselves without having a herder or cattlemen to see to their daily needs. Along our roads and highways you will see signs that display a cow. This means that you could encounter one of these independent beasts right on the highway. Just in the last month or two we have had two deadly traffic accidents right here on this highway going through Abiquiú. The unsuspecting driver encountered cattle on the road, causing the deadly accident—both to the driver and travel companions and also to the cows.

Free Range areas can be found in most cattle states. However, our Native American culture taught us that land was sacred and the land of the Southwest was not something to be possessed, but was something to be cherished and honored. We had always thought that the land we could see around us belongs to all natives living here. Land grants followed by settlers who fenced in their property were a concept that we found hard to embrace.

I recall a story told to me when I was a little kid about a man who lived as a hermit in a cabin high up in the mountains above Abiquiú. We called him The Mountain Man. He was seldom seen but he did come down to the village once in while to visit the store and the saloon. He had a herd of cattle that had the unusualy characteristic of giving birth to twin calves each season. However, the ranchers who had turned their cattle loose into these mountains had the unfortunate luck of having cows that were barren. When they went to get their cows they would find that there were no calves born this year.

The cattle were so used to this independent routine that, if the rancher was late in coming for them in the fall, they would find their own way down from the mountain into the village. Same thing would happen the next spring when the ranchers would turn them loose for summer grazing in the mountains; they knew where to go and they would take off and head for their green pastures.

The ranchers are supposed to keep the cows out of the village, but sometimes they let them wander into the homes along the creek and then the cows will make their way up into the village. I have had to make sure that my gate is closed when roaming cows have been spotted in the village. One time there were four big bulls fighting right in the middle of the village. What a time to have a good movie camera available! But I didn't even have a disposable camera with which to document this event.

Right now there are two goats running loose up on the Abiquiú Mesa. These were my goats at one time, but I sold them to my cousin and then they got away from him. They still can be seen up there. It was two or three years ago that they turned themselves loose to fend for themselves.

The Rescue

When my cousin, Augustin, was about 13 or 14 he rode up into the mountains behind his home in Abiquiú to check on the cows that his family had wintering up there. He took his single-shot 22 rifle with him just in case he saw a rabbit or a deer. This really wasn't a task for him because this is what he loved to do—ride his horse up into the mountains and hunt rabbits or deer. He told his mother that he was going up into the mountains to look after the cattle, so she knew about where he was going to be—in an area that we call *Frioles*.

There was about two feet of snow on the ground. He was riding around with his loaded gun looking for something to shoot. Somehow the gun slipped from his hand, fell to the ground and discharged—hitting him right in his belly. He held on to the horse as well as he could, but he was beginning to feel dizzy. He eventually fell from the horse right at the edge of a little gully. His horse stood nearby while Augustin tried to stand up. But instead of walking towards the horse, he fell backwards and rolled down into the gully. He tried to crawl out of the gully, but he couldn't. That's about all that Augustin remembers, so he must have passed out at that point. The horse found its way back to the house and stood at the gate to the corral.

My dad, who was Augustin's uncle, was staying with his brother at that time. My dad was a drifter and a drunk. But this day he was not drunk. He saw the horse over by the corral and went and told Augustin's mother. She told him where Augustin had planned to ride that day, so my Dad got on a horse and went to find Augustin.

He went about eight or ten miles up into Frioles Canyon, following the horse's tracks in the snow. He looked all around and finally heard Augustin hollering. Augustin doesn't remember yelling, but he must have. My dad found him, and Augustin was almost frozen. He was afraid to put him on the horse because he could see that he was shot and feared the ride would make things worse. He covered Augustin with his jacket, then hurried back to the home of Joe Ferran, who had a truck that could go up into the mountains to bring Augustin down.

They were able to bring Augustin home, where they put him into a tub of snow—that is what you do to folks who suffer from frostbite, then you rub them all over to get their blood circulating again. An ambulance came and took him to the hospital. He survived the bullet wound, but lost some of his fingertips and toes.

I like telling this story because it tells a good story about my dad. He did not live with his brother, but would sleep in one of the outbuildings when he was in the village. He was usually drunk, but this day he was not. He was able to use some of the hunting and tracking skills that he had learned as a boy growing up in these mountains to find Augustin and save his life. This is a nice memory to have of Dad.

What to See and Do in Abiquiú

Abiquiú is located about 46 miles from Santa Fe, northwest on Highway 84. After passing through the town of Española, the scenery begins to change drastically. Small ranches and clusters of trailers give way to giant mesas of red and white cliffs. Abiquiú is located on a bend in the Chama River.

About a mile and half before arriving in Abiquiú one will pass a church ruin on the right. This is Santa Rosa de Lima, the original church for the village when it was located down

Napoleón Garcia, Tourist Information and Guide, 2007. Photo by Analinda

closer to the river. If you stop here please respect the signs regarding visitation. The location of the village was too hard to defend, so it was moved up on the mesa where it stands today. We celebrate our Spanish heritage in late August with a festival that begins at Santa Rosa de Lima, and then we walk up to St. Tomás Church in the village. In November we celebrate our Indian heritage at St. Tomas Church with a two-day festival that includes much beating of the drums and dancing.

The village of Abiquiú is tucked away, up a hill, past the Post Office. Many people come to Abiquiú and think that Bode's store on Highway 84 and the Post Office are all that there is to Abiquiú. Be aware that some local people may tell you that you are not welcomed in the village of Abiquiú and perhaps some busybody will stop you and tell you this. However, that is not true. You are welcome. In the spirit of Miss O'Keeffe when we would be out driving and I might caution her that maybe we shouldn't be entering a certain area she would say, "Go on, Paul. If they stop us we will just leave."

Be venturesome and drive up County Road 187, into the plaza. The first house you see on your right is a private residence. Next to this house on your right is the building that used to be the old Bode store. Bode moved the store down to the highway when the new Highway 84 was built. The home behind the adobe wall on your left is the Georgia O'Keeffe Home and Studio.

The O'Keeffe home is a large Colonial-style home sitting on about four acres. The home overlooks the Chama River Valley. Actually, you can see the home before you arrive in Abiquiú. The large glass window in her bedroom has an excellent view of the valley and the Sangre de Cristo Mountains in the distance. You can even see the peaks near Taos from the edge of her mesa. Tours are given March through October on Tuesday, Thursday, and Friday. The Tour Office is next to the

Abiquiú Inn on the highway between Santa Rosa de Lima Church and Bode's store. Reservations are a must and should be made a month or two in advance of visiting Abiquiú.

Continuing on into the plaza and after passing the old store you will see St. Tomás Catholic Church on your right. On your left is a typical New Mexican rundown adobe building. This building was the clinic that Georgia O'Keeffe helped to establish. We have a new clinic now, down on the highway near Bode's store. You are now in the Abiquiú Plaza. The library is on your right, just across from the church. They are usually open Sunday through Thursday from 1-6 pm. Yes, there is computer access if you just have to check your eMail.

When entering the Plaza you will notice a rich man's home up in the far left corner. That is the Bode home. The poor man's home just to the left of it is my home. If my Open signs are out, please stop in and say "Hello".

Plaza Blanca, 2006. Photo by Analinda

The drive around the village is about one mile and well worth the time. Turn right in front of the church and wind your way past the library and up the hill. The road will take you past many old and new homes in the village. You will pass the old, seldom used, Moquí *morada*, pass our fire station, keep to your left and continue on up and around until you get to the cemetery. Now you are on your way back down. Driving in this direction will give you the wonderful view of the Chama River Valley. To your right is the Abiquiú Mesa, blocking your view of the Sangre de Cristo Mountains in the distance. From here you can see the White Cliffs, or *Plaza Blanca*, across the valley. Georgia O'Keeffe frequently painted these cliffs. She called them *The White Place*. She also visited and painted an area that she called *The Black Place*; however, that location is about 150 miles northwest of Abiquiú towards Farmington and the Four Corners area.

Plaza Blanca, 2006. Photo by Analinda

Soon, you will pass the *Morada del Alto* on your right, the active *morada* in Abiquiú. As requested at the Santa Rosa de Lima Church, please respect this sacred site. At the bottom of the hill you will turn left and head back to the plaza, completing you circle tour. When you turned left you will pass the O'Keeffe Home and Studio on your right. Notice the water ditch along the wall. This is the ditch that brings the precious water from the mountains that O'Keeffe so desired for her garden.

The road in front of the O'Keeffe home is the original road through Abiquiú. It continued on past the side of the old store, down the hill, and then on to the village of Barranco, then followed the Chama River on northward. Do not turn right when you come down the hill from the *morada*! The old road is barely passable in that direction as it goes down and connects to Highway 84.

You can tour further up the mountains behind Abiquiú. After returning to Highway 84, turn left and then left again at the first road, County Road 189. This takes you past some very old Abiquiú homes, then past newer homes before you reach where the paved road gives way to dirt. This road goes through the Abiquiú Grant; however, it also is a forest access road, so you are permitted to travel on it. You will pass the rock memorial on your left to the early Spanish settlers who lost their lives in an Indian raid in the early 1800s. When you reach the part of the spring where two creeks join, pull off into the parking area and enjoy this bit of nature. Here is where the watercress grows year round. I often drove Miss O'Keeffe here with her visitors. If you continue on up to your left you will soon be on top of the Abiquiú Mesa and treated to my ancestral views of our Grant.

About six miles north of Abiquiú off Highway 96, you will find Abiquiú Lake, a reservoir on the Chama River. It is managed by the Corps of Engineers and there is a lovely campground with electricity, water, and hot showers. The campground is in operation from April 15 until October 1. Bordering the lake is the majestic Cerro Pedernal, the mountain that appears in so many O'Keeffe paintings.

Further north, about 15 miles from Abiquiú, is Ghost Ranch, the dude ranch where Georgia O'Keeffe first stayed and where she bought a home in 1940. It is now owned by the Presbyterian Church, but is open to visitors. They provide an O'Keeffe Landscape Tour where they will take you on a minivan around the area pointing out the vistas that ended up on her canvases. Tours are held mid-March to mid-November, Tuesday, Thursday, Friday and Saturday at 1:30 pm. Ghost Ranch offers a variety of workshops and is a popular retreat center. The O'Keeffe Museum now owns the O'Keeffe home, *Rancho de los Burros*, but it is not open to the public nor is it visible from the Ghost Ranch.

Cerro Pedernal provides the backdrop for the very popular recreation spot — Abiquiú Lake, 2006. Photo by Analinda

There are three museums at Ghost Ranch: Florence Hawley Ellis Museum of Anthropology, Ruth Hall Museum of Paleontology and back on the highway, continuing north, you will find the Ghost Ranch Piedra Lumbre Education and Visitor's Center. This latter museum was originally planned as a desert wildlife museum, but that effort was moved to Tucson and became the very popular Arizona Sonora Desert Museum. The Visitor's Center at Ghost Ranch now has exhibits of local interest and an occasional art show or book signing. This is a good spot for photographing the red cliffs of Ghost Ranch.

Just a little further north on Highway 84 you will come to Forest Road 151 on your left. This will take you to the Rio Chama Wilderness Area. The Rio Chama Wilderness encompasses 50,300 acres in northwest New Mexico. The U.S. Department of Agriculture designated the land a wilderness area in 1978; and in 1986 the Rio Chama, that flows through the wilderness, was deemed a Wild and Scenic River. The very narrow, one lane road winds up and down along the Chama River. There are areas for camping, rafting and boating. After about 12 or 13 miles you will come to the Christ in the Desert Monastery. This lovely Benedictine monastery was built in the 1970s. It provides a quiet retreat for the weary travelers in a remote area surrounded by the Rio Chama Wilderness. They are open to the public and there is a very nice gift shop and book store. My father-in-law, Joe Ferran, was the contractor who built the unique church that is designed to blend in with the surrounding cliffs. My brother and oldest son, Leo, also helped with this construction. They had to travel each day on that winding road, which was worse then, to work on the church. In good weather, it is a good road, but in bad weather, it is a bad road. It is very narrow with little or no shoulders or pullouts for passing oncoming cars. There have been recent improvements, but please don't try it in wet or snowy weather— it can be very hazardous.

Continuing north on Highway 84 you will come to Echo Amphitheater on your left. This is a natural walled arena of sandstone that creates an echo chamber.. The area is managed by the Carson National Forest. There is a Day Use picnic area available with picnic tables and toilets.

Echo Ampitheater, 2006. Photo by Analinda

Hiking in and around Abiquiú

Ghost Ranch has many hiking trails. Check in at the reception desk for maps.

Poshuouinge Ruins, about 2.5 miles south of Abiquiú on highway 84, just past Trujillo's Store. Poshuouinge is managed by the Santa Fe National Forest. The trail is half-mile in length with two vista areas and interpretive signs. The trail traverses steep, uneven surfaces and overlooks remnants of an old pueblo and the Chama River Valley. The principal ruins include a large pueblo with over 700 ground-floor rooms surrounding two large plazas with a large kiva in the larger plaza. Parking is provided along the highway. At the top of your hike you will be able to obtain cell phone reception. There is no cell phone reception within about a two-mile radius of the village of Abiquiú. Perhaps those witches are still at work.

Another nearby hiking opportunity would be **Plaza Blanca or the White Cliffs**, a frequent backdrop for many O'Keeffe paintings (she called it The White Place). It is located on the grounds of the Dar al Islam Mosque. Take County Road 155 to your right just north of Abiquiú, after crossing the Chama River. Continue for about three miles on this dirt road that winds along the Chama River. The sign to the mosque and Plaza Blanca will be on the left. As you drive up their drive the road to the mosque will split off to the left, stay on the road that goes to the right and soon you will come to a parking place. Visitors are welcome to gently walk and admire this beautiful canyon on Dar al Islam lands. For workshops, commercial photography and filming, you must contact the mosque office. If their gate is open you are welcome to visit. As in many sacred places found in the Chama River Valley, please respect their visitation rules.

Hiking Cerro Pedernal - *Pedernal* means flint in Spanish. Natives living nearby during the Pueblo Period, 1303-1324, used Pedernal's stone for arrowheads, scrapers, knives, and spear points. "It is my private mountain," O'Keeffe once said, "God told me if I painted it enough, I could have it." She did indeed include this mountain in many of her paintings and her ashes were scattered on its top. Perdernal rises majestically over the Chama Valley; its sloping cone, topped by a long flat ridge of lava, is visible on the horizon from northwest of Santa Fe and can be seen from as far away as Taos.

Elevation of Pedernal is about 8000'. Difficulty of the hike is difficult to strenuous, rated as a Class 3 from the base of the cliff to its top. Duration is about 3-4 hours for the seven miles round trip hike. It is managed by the Santa Fe National Forest.

To reach Pedernal take Highway 96 off Highway 84, towards Abiquiú Lake. When entering the village of Youngsville turn left onto Forest Road F100. Follow gravel road for 5.7 miles, turn left onto F160 and follow dirt road past gate. Look for parking or drive the dirt road all the way to a plain field below the base of the cliffs. A high clearance vehicle is useful. There are no marked trails. Two primitive trails ascend to the cliffs.

Abiquiú Annual Events

Abiquiú Farm Tour takes place in mid-July. This two-day event features Abiquiú farms specializing in wine grapes, lavender, livestock, produce and fruit. Each farm has a separate venue showcasing crafts, food and their indigenous products.

Fiesta of Santa Rosa de Lima is celebrated each year on August 30 and begins with the carrying of the statue of Santa Rosa to Santo Tomás Church. This procession begins at the church ruins on Highway 84 and ends at the Church in the village. There are local food and craft booths around the plaza. Music and dancing goes on all day in the plaza. this is the time when the Genízaros in Abiquiú get to celebrate their Spanish heritage.

The **Annual Abiquiú Studio Art Tour** takes place on Columbus Day weekend in October. A self-guided, driving tour takes you to over 50 artists who open their studios to the public to show and sell their art. You can experience the unique artistry of the region and enjoy local food while enjoying the spectacular fall landscape. I'm at stop #17 in the Abiquiú Plaza. Come by and see my woodcarvings and visit for a while.

In late November we celebrate our Indian heritage. This annual **Abiquiú Feast Day** includes San Juan pueblo singers and Tewa dances done by young *Abiqueños* wearing costumes that celebrate the village's ancient Native American traditions. Good food and dancing are key elements of this fiesta.

Abiquiú Lodgings

Abiquiú Inn - Hwy 84. Offers gracious southwest accommodations with full service restaurant, gift shop and gallery. 505-685-4178 www.Abiquiúinn.com

Ghost Ranch Bed and Breakfast - Comfortable accommodations at a variety of price ranges to fit your budget. Enjoy spectacular views of the red clay hills of O'Keeffe Country. 505-685-4333 or 877-804-4678. www.ghostranch.org.

Las Parras de Abiquiú R&B - Hwy 84. Offers a separate casita with two spacious bedrooms. All the luxuries—fireplaces, king-size beds, and hot tub. 505-685-4200 www.lasparras.com

Old Abiquiú Bed & Breakfast - Hwy 84. A memorable adobe overlooking a shelered cove and an ancient cottonwood tree on the Rio Chama. 505-685-4784

El Cencerro Bed and Breakfast - County Road 155 right across from the entrance to Dar al Islam Mosque. Nestled on the banks of the Chama River, El Cencerro is built in pueblo style, with walls more than a foot thick built with strawbale infill. El Cencerro is situated amidst beautiful old cottonwood trees on 22 acres of land. 505-685-4100 www.elcencerro.us/

Abiquiú Restaurants

Abiquiú Inn - Hwy 84. Full Service Restaurant 505-685-4378

Bode's Store -Hwy 84. Deli style food, snacks and cold drinks

Trujillo's Country Store - Hwy 84. Snacks and cold drinks

Alternate Route - Scenic Tour

If you have time to explore, take Highway 84 to Tierra Amarilla to Highway 64 back to Taos. If you continue on to Chama on Highway 84 you could visit the Tierra Wools in Los Ojos, a weaver/spinner/grower-owed company. Tierra Wools offers a glimpse of a time when the Hispanic weaving tradition maintained village artisans through long cold winters. Today, the worker-owned company helps insure that sheepherding and weaving continue to preserve our land and culture. Guest lodgings are provided for their weaving school.

In Chama you can take a ride on the Cumbres and Toltec Scenic Railroad, a steam train ride that goes from Chama to Antonito, Colorado. Hidden away in a little-known corner of the southern Rocky Mountains is a historic artifact of the American West that time forgot. Built in 1880 and little changed since, the Cumbres & Toltec Scenic Railroad is the finest and most spectacular example of steam era mountain railroading in North America. Its equipment, structures and vast landscape exist today as if frozen in the first half of the 20th century. The Cumbres & Toltec Scenic Railroad operates seven days a week, starting at the end of May and continuing through mid-October. Several times during the year they provide holiday trips for families.

Resources

Abiquiú Lake Recreation Area-U.S. Army Corps of
Engineers -www.spa.usace.army.mil/recreation/ab/
index.htm

Abiquiú Studio Art Tour - www.Abiquiustudiotour.org/

Chama River Wilderness, Santa Fe National Forest - www.
fs.fed.us/r3/sfe/recreation/wilderness.htm#chama

Christ in the Desert Monastery - http://christdesert.org/

Cumbres and Toltec Scenic Railroad - 1-888-CUMBRES
http://www.cumbrestoltec.com/

Digital Abiquiú, community portal for Abiquiú - www.
digitalAbiquiu.com/

Echo Amphitheater, Carson National Forest - www.fs.fed.
us/r3/carson/recreation/trails/trail-descriptions/trail_
echo_canyon.shtml

Ghost Ranch Education and Retreat Center -
505-685-4333 www.ghostranch.org/

O'Keeffe Landscape Tour at Ghost Ranch - 505-685-4333
www.ghostranch.org

O'Keeffe Home and Studio Tour - 505-685-4539 www.
okeeffemuseum.org

Plaza Blanca and Dar al Islam Mosque - 800-447-5621 or
505-685-4515

**Santa Rosa de Lima Ruin and St. Tomás Apostle Church
Parish** - 505-685-4462

Tierra Wools - 575-588-7231 www.handweavers.com

Tourist Information and Guided Tours - Napoleón
Garcia, on the Plaza in Abiquiú. 505-685-4613

Napoleón Garcia feeding his flock of homing pigeons in his backyard, 2006. Photo by Analinda

About the Authors

After completing 30 years with the Federal Civil Service in Washington, D.C in computer technology, Analinda Dunn began a 15-year career in elementary education. She traveled the Lewis and Clark Trail during the recent Bicentennial Commemoration events of 2003-2006 in her 16-foot travel trailer, journaling and documenting her adventure. She fell in love with this mode of travel and began to travel full time with the goal of traveling the historic trails of America's western movement. This travel led her to northern New Mexico where she fell under the enchantment of the state and now makes Abiquiú her home. She considers living in northern New Mexico to be an ideal location to further her study of American history and to explore actual historic trails and sites.

Napoleón Garcia is a *Genízaro* native of Abiquiú, New Mexico. A *Genízaro* native claims ancestry of both the Colonial Spanish settlers and Native American Indian tribes of the area. He has a small gallery in his home where he works and displays his woodcarving skills. He also provides tourist information, local tours of the area, maps of local points of interest and good conversation of local lore. Native folklore, area history, and personal tales of growing up and living in a remote village in northern New Mexico provide the substance of the stories that Napoleón likes to tell. He also knew and worked for the artist, Georgia O'Keeffe, who lived the last 40 years of her life in his village, just "around the corner".

CPSIA information can be obtained at www.ICGtesting.com
Printed in the USA
BVOW07s0215280515

402013BV00003B/516/P